# JAZZ CLASSICS
## FOR GUITAR TAB

ISBN 978-1-4803-9444-5

HAL•LEONARD®
CORPORATION
7777 W. BLUEMOUND RD. P.O. BOX 13819 MILWAUKEE, WI 53213

Visit Hal Leonard Online at
**www.halleonard.com**

# Afternoon In Paris

BY JOHN LEWIS

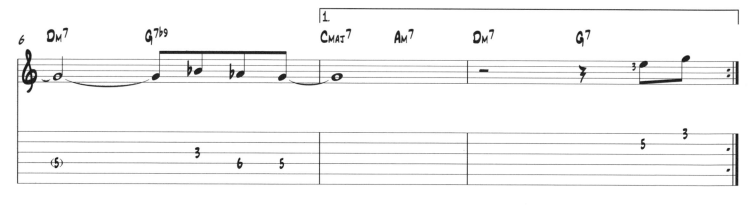

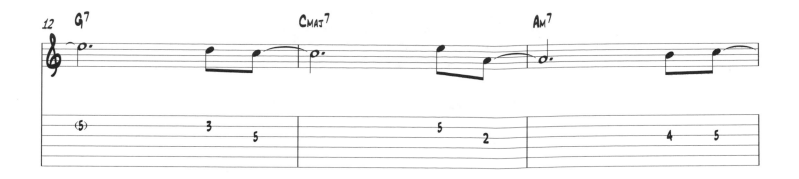

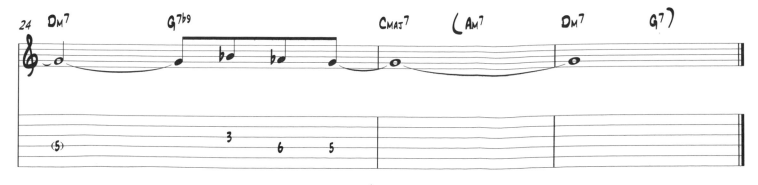

# Ain't Misbehavin'

FROM AIN'T MISBEHAVIN'

Words by Andy Razaf
Music by Thomas "Fats" Waller and Harry Brooks

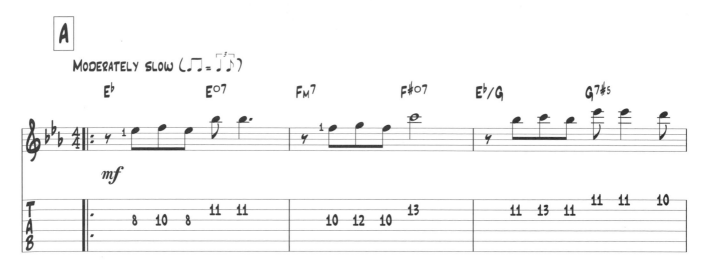

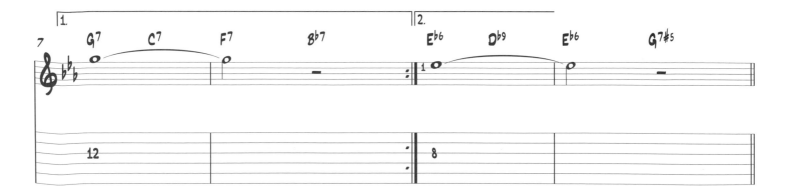

# All of Me

Words and Music by Seymour Simons and Gerald Marks

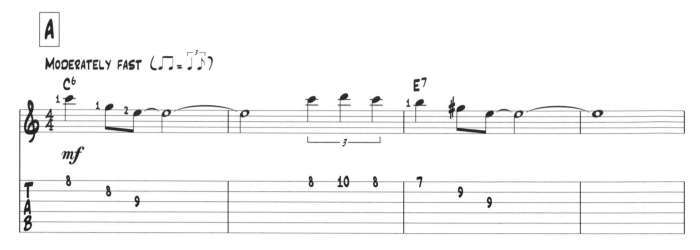

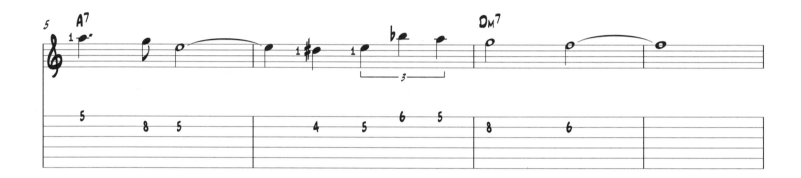

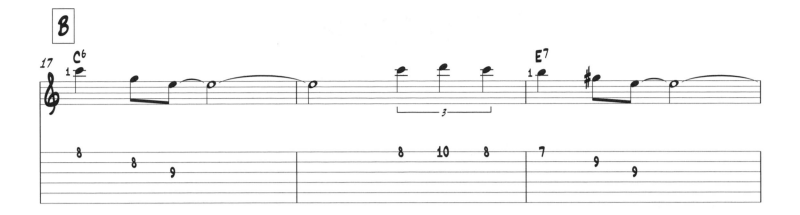

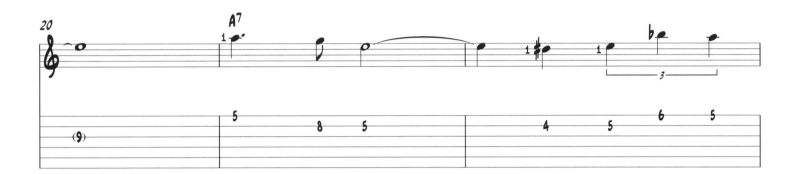

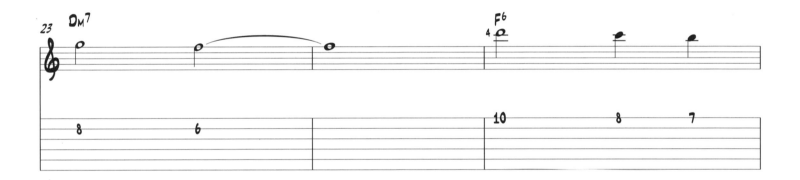

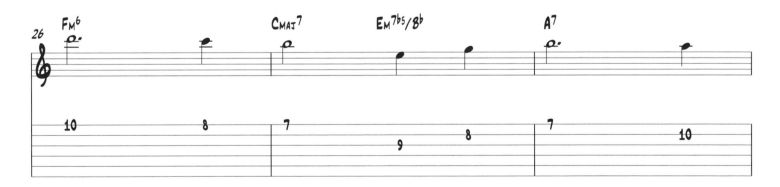

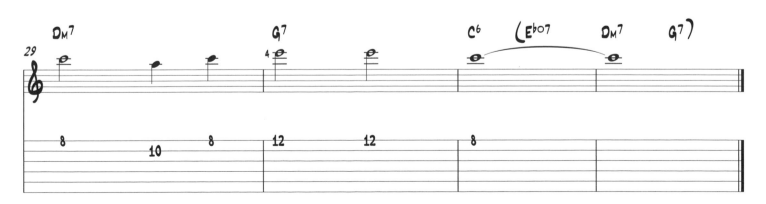

# ANTHROPOLOGY

By Charlie Parker and Dizzy Gillespie

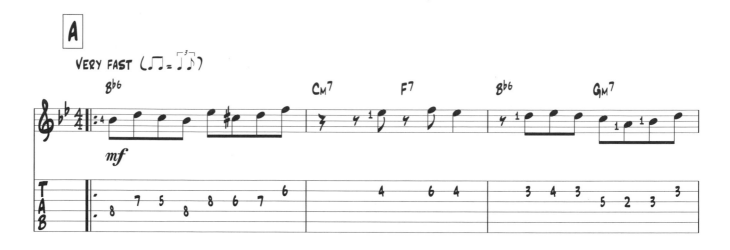

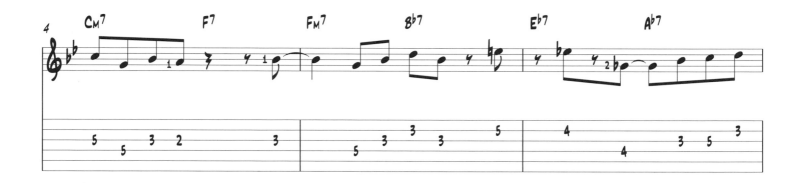

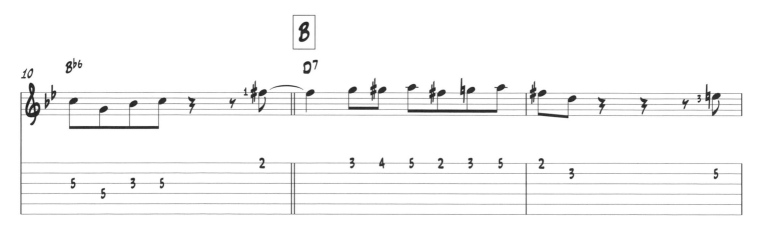

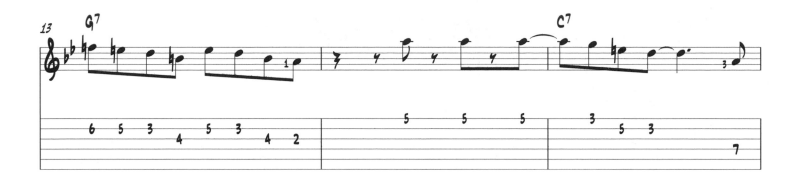

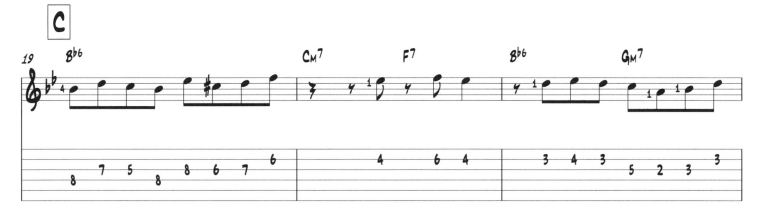

# Au Privave

By Charlie Parker

# Billie's Bounce
## (Bill's Bounce)

By Charlie Parker

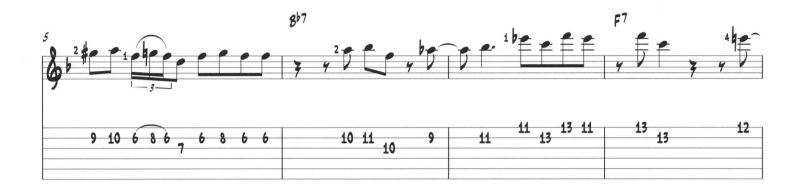

# Autumn in New York

Words and Music by Vernon Duke

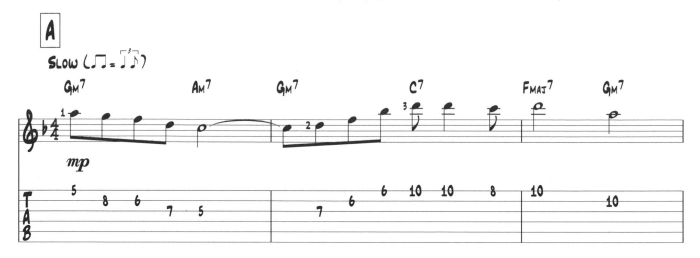

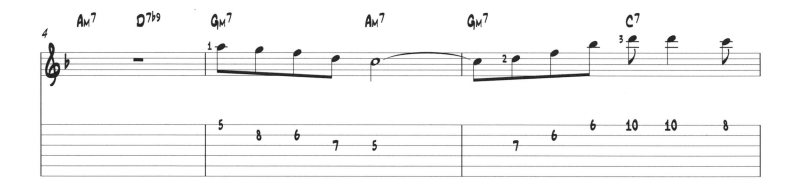

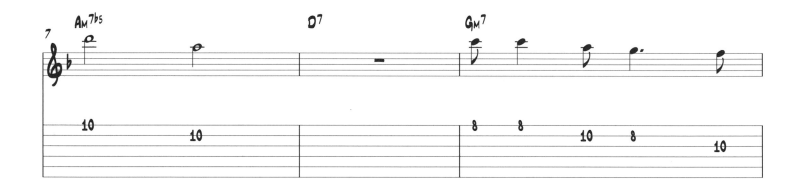

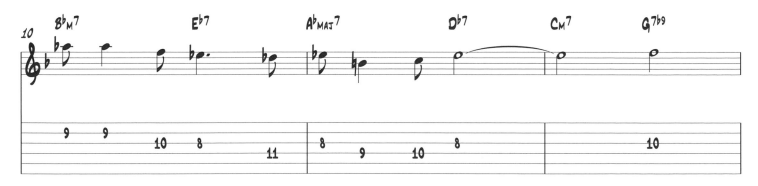

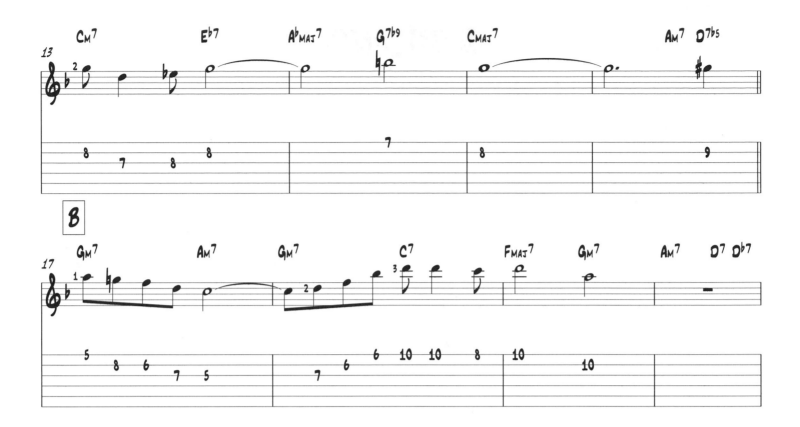

# Birdland

## By Josef Zawinul

INTRO

Moderately fast

*Synth bass arr. for gtr.

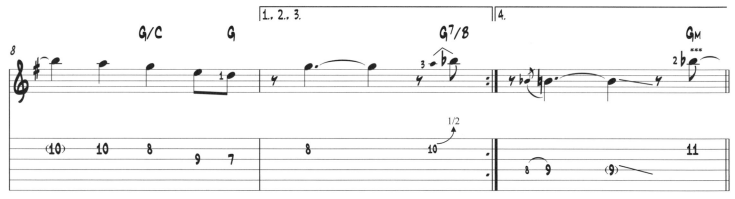

**Bass arr. for gtr.

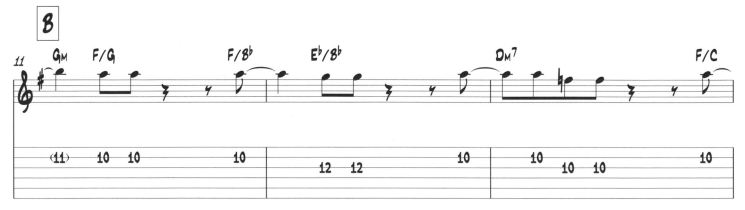

***Sax arr. for gtr.

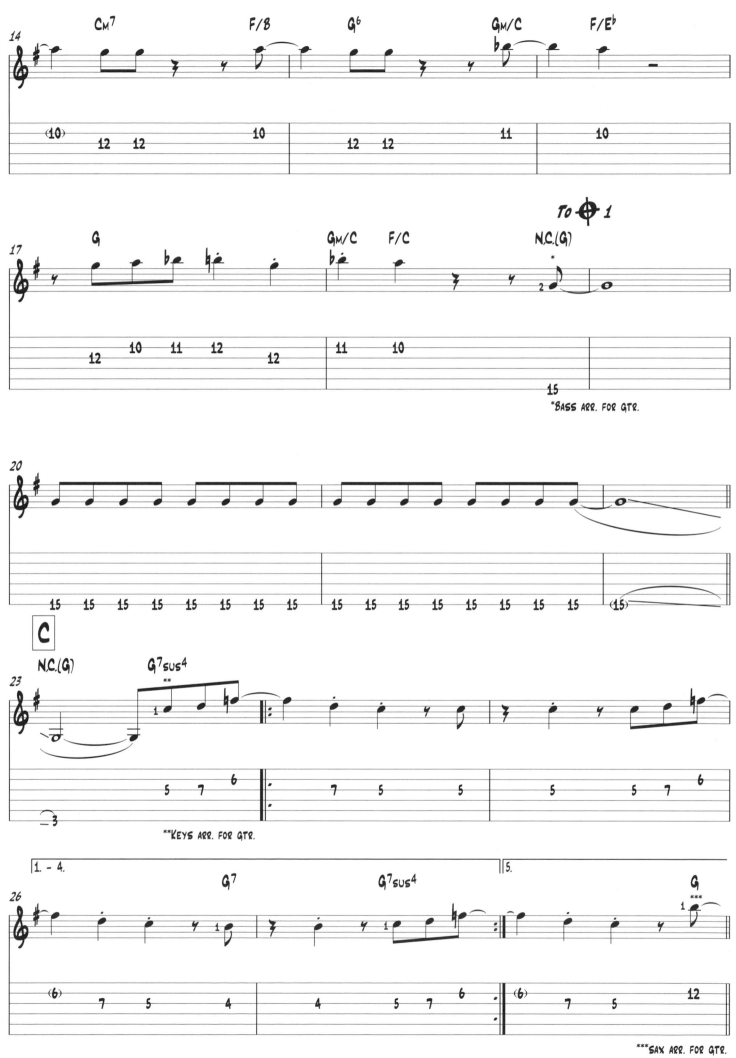

*Bass arr. for gtr.

**Keys arr. for gtr.

***Sax arr. for gtr.

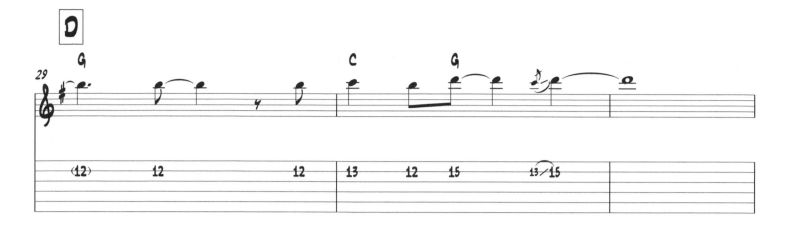

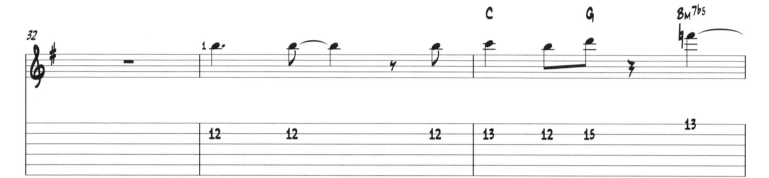

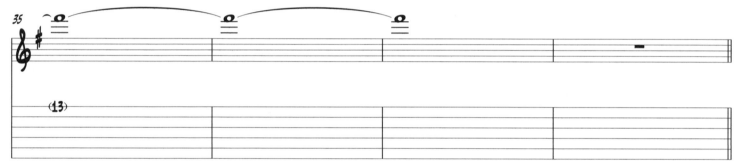

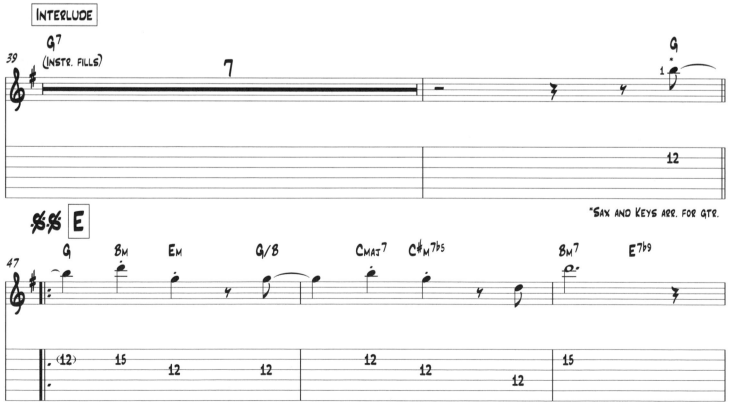

*Synth bass arr. for gtr.

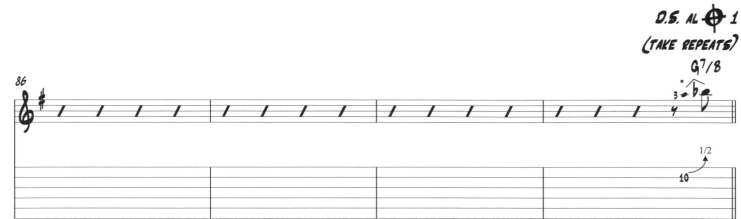

*BASS ARR. FOR GTR.

# Confirmation

By Charlie Parker

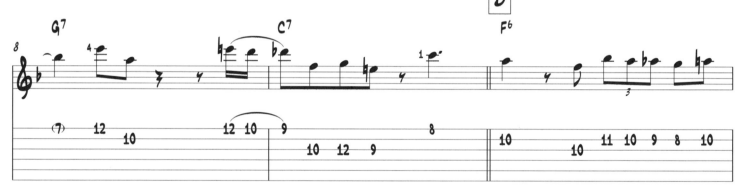

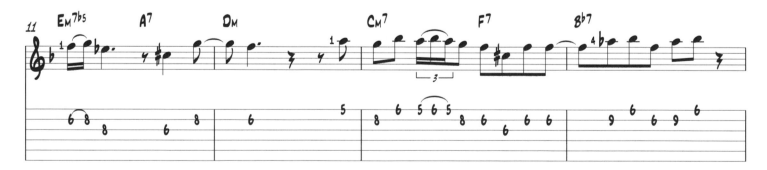

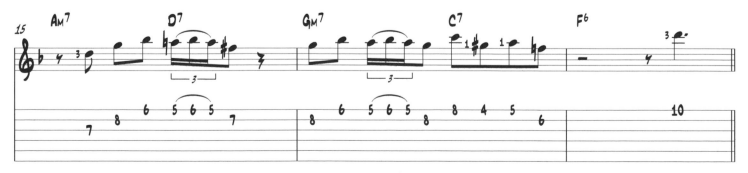

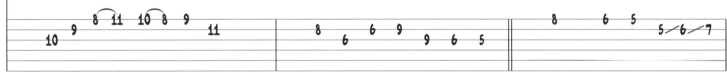

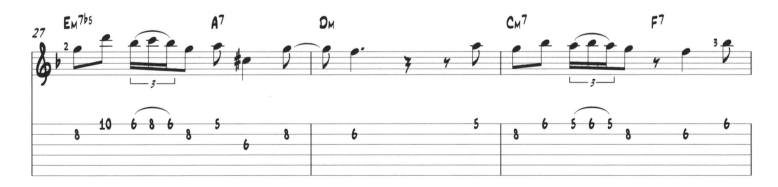

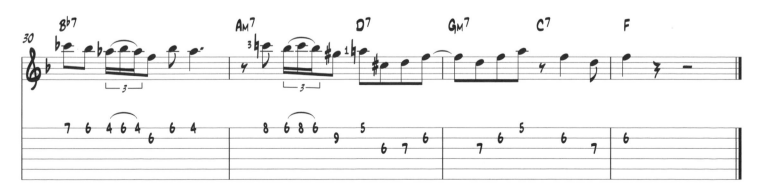

# Darling Lili

Words by Johnny Mercer
Music by Henry Mancini

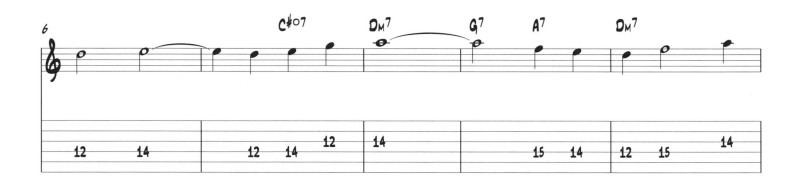

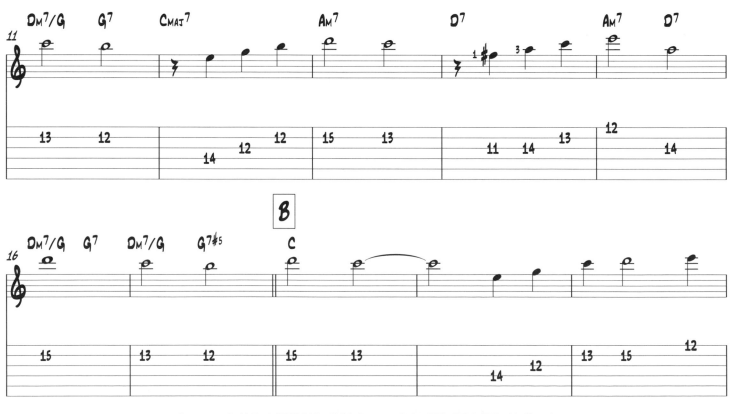

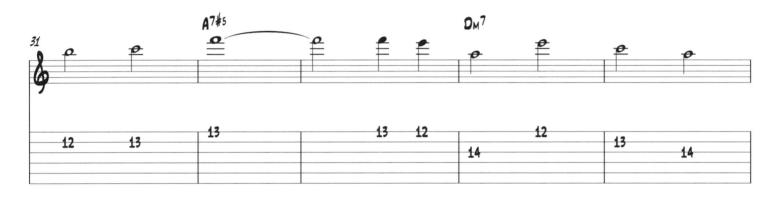

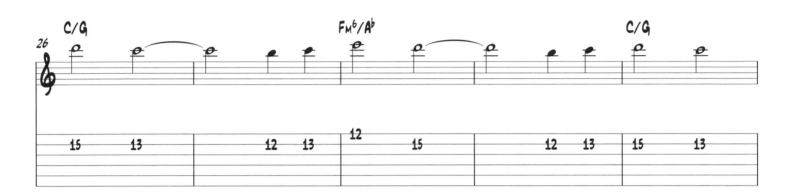

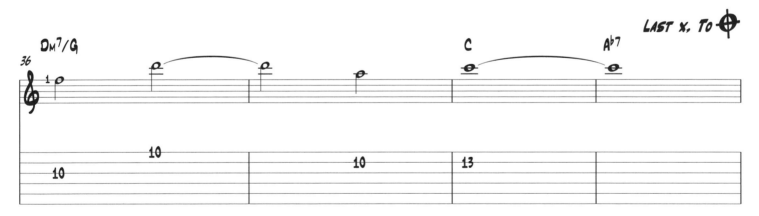

# Dolphin Dance

By Herbie Hancock

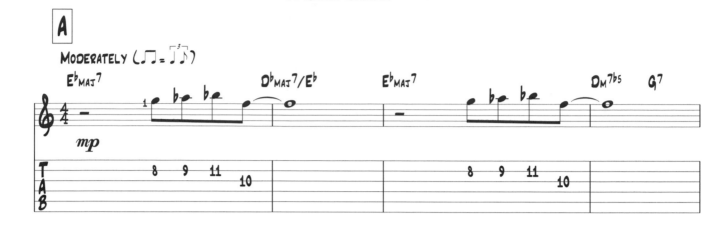

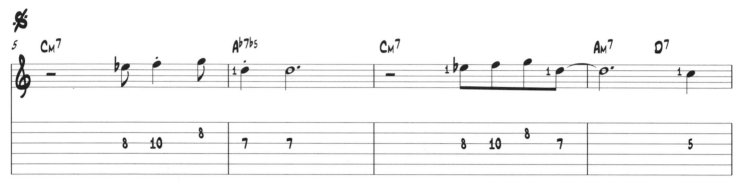

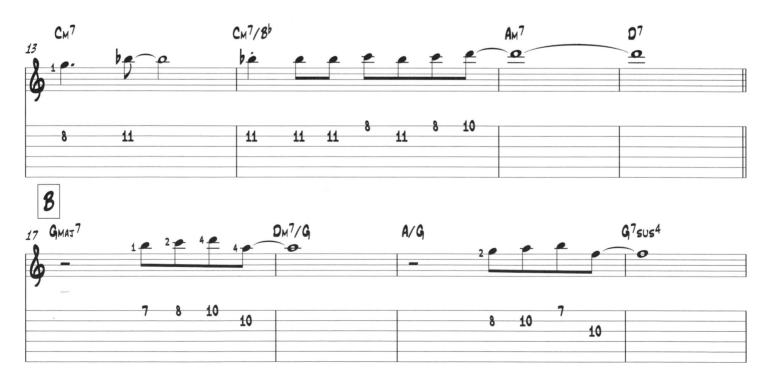

# Don't Get Around Much Anymore

Featured in **SOPHISTICATED LADIES**

Words and Music by Duke Ellington and Bob Russell

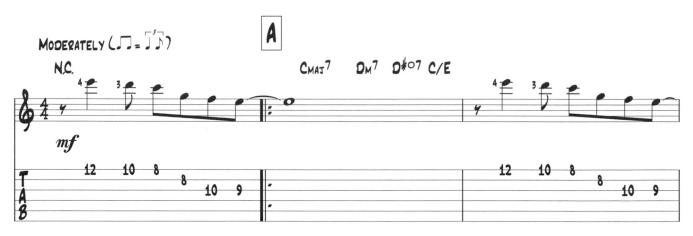

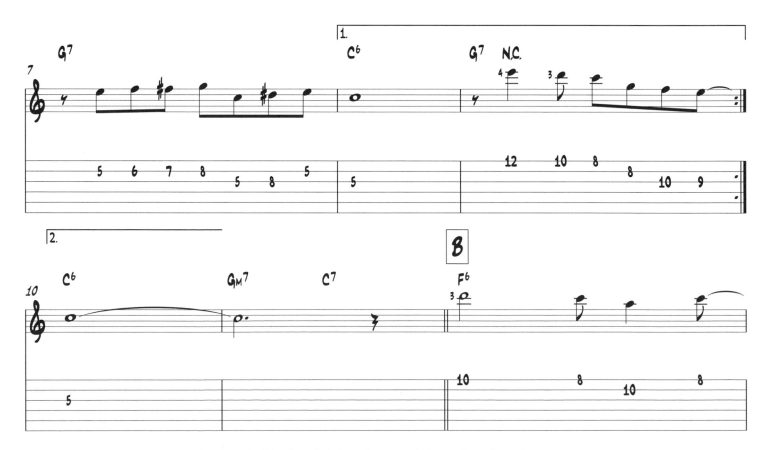

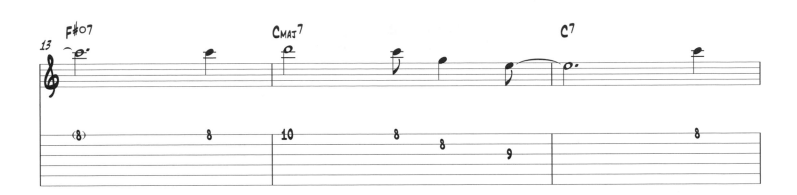

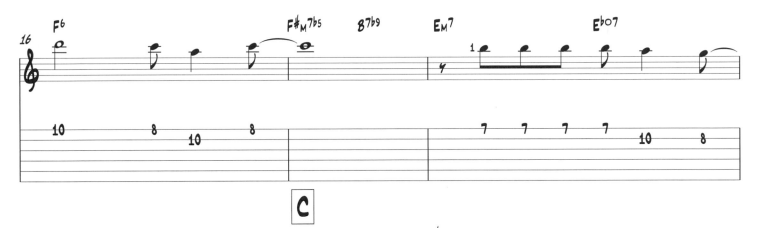

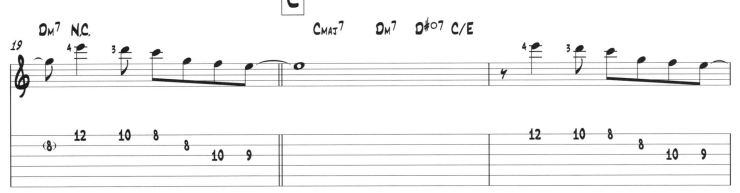

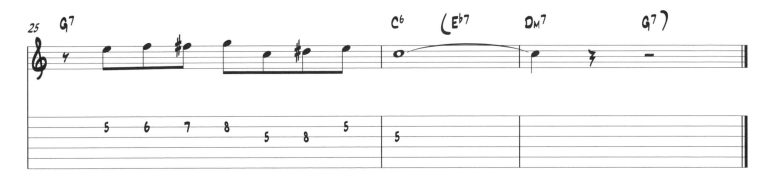

# Donna Lee

## By Charlie Parker

A

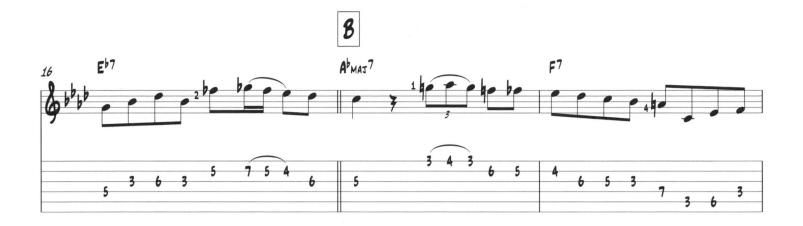

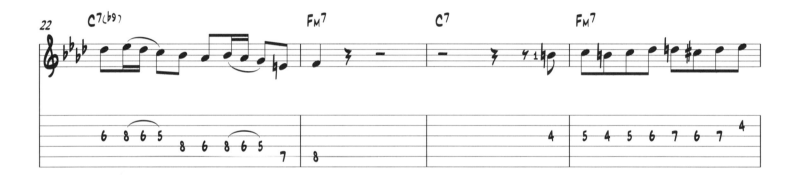

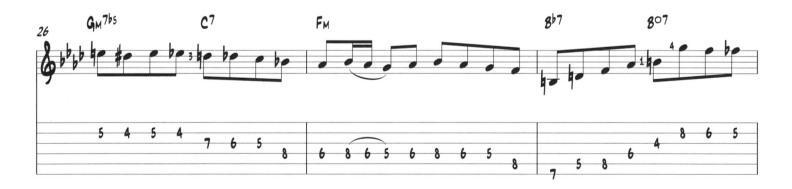

# Doxy

By Sonny Rollins

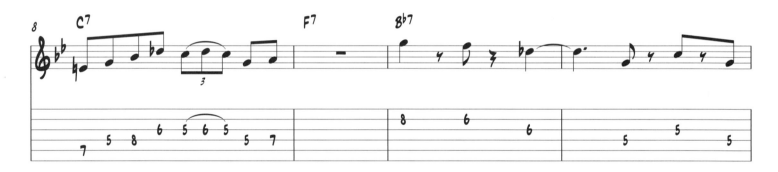

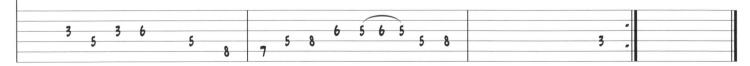

# Footprints

By Wayne Shorter

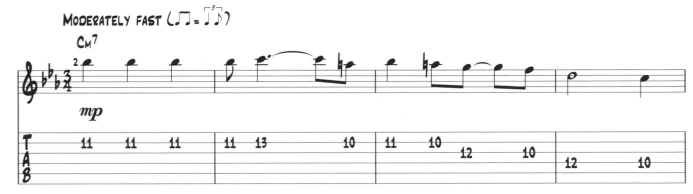

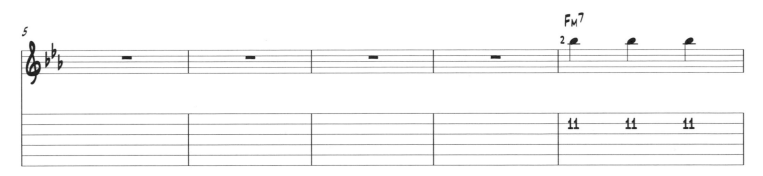

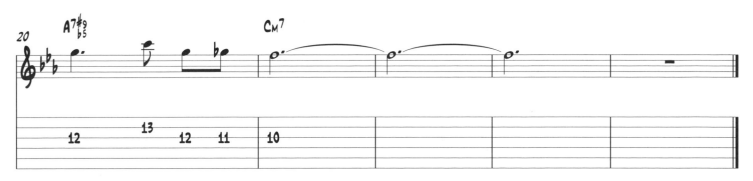

# Epistrophy

By Thelonious Monk and Kenny Clarke

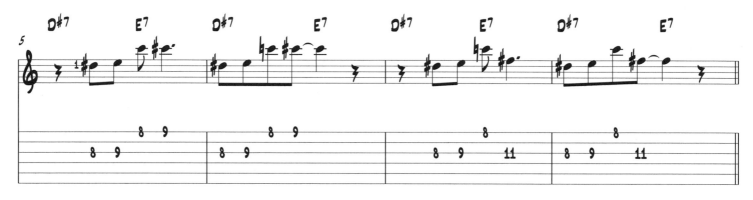

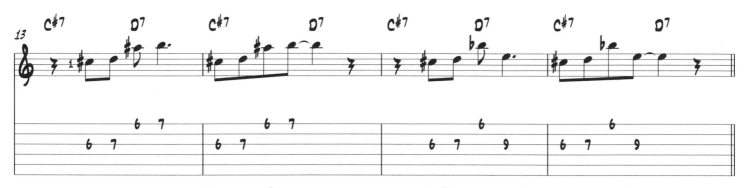

AFTER SOLOS, D.C. AL

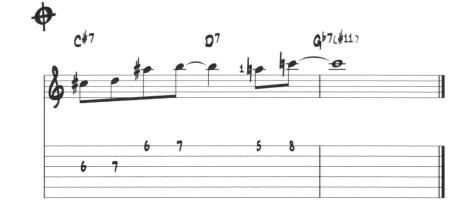

# Fascinating Rhythm

### from Rhapsody in Blue

### Music and Lyrics by George Gershwin and Ira Gershwin

**A**

Moderately slow, in 2

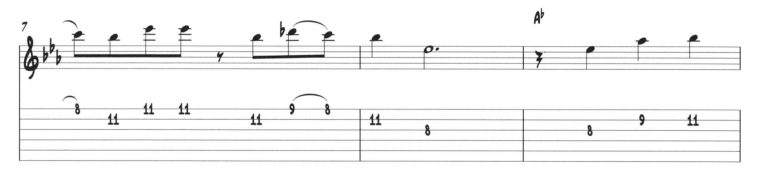

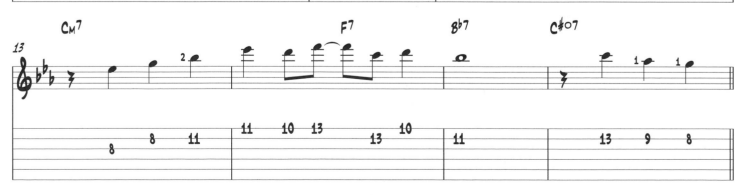

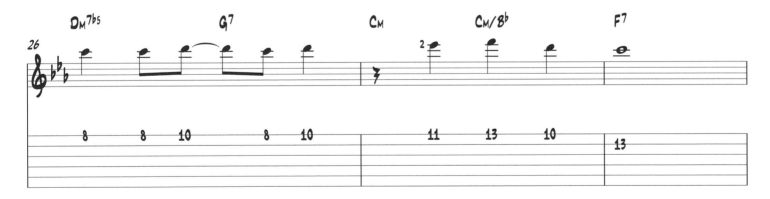

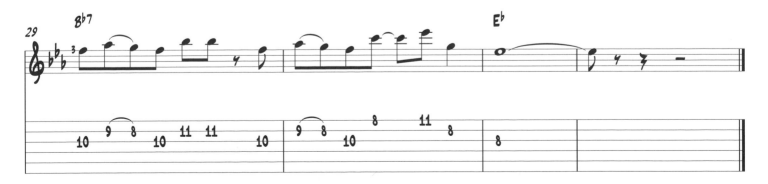

# Fly Me to the Moon
## (In Other Words)

Featured in the Motion Picture ONCE AROUND

Words and Music by Bart Howard

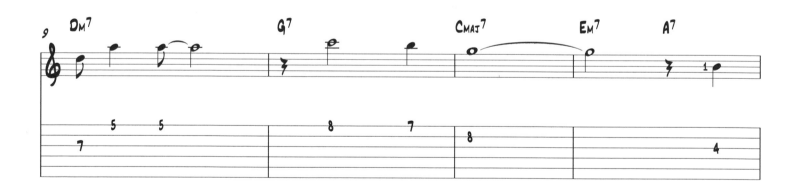

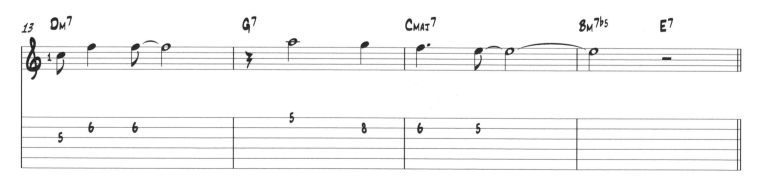

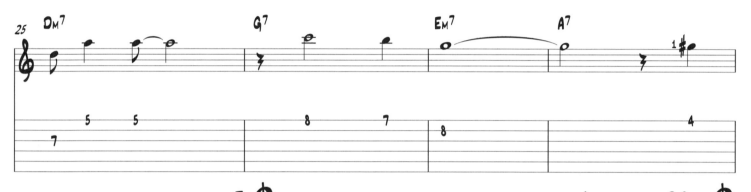

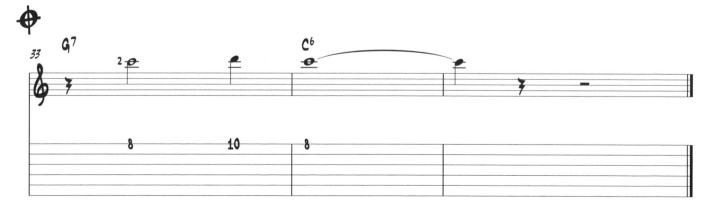

# Four

## By Miles Davis

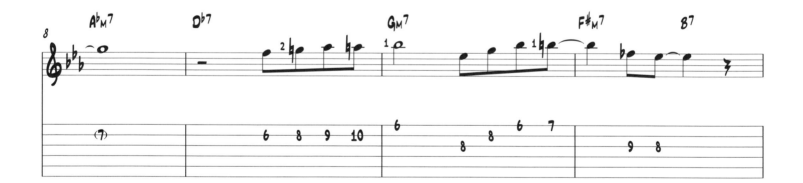

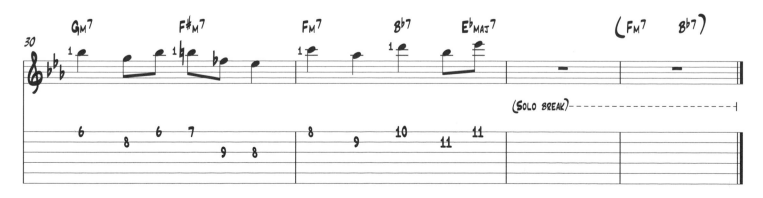

39

# Four on Six

By John L. (Wes) Montgomery

*Chord symbols reflect implied harmony.

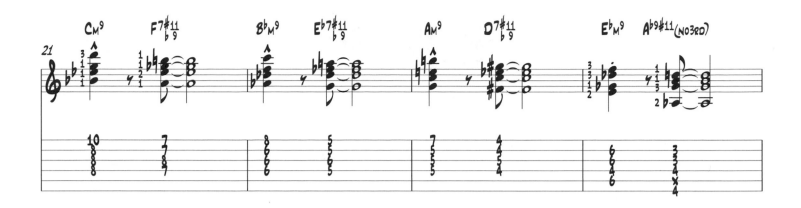

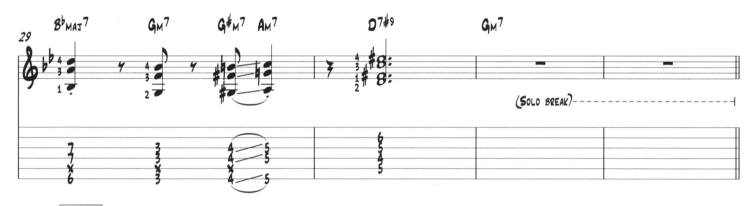

**SOLOS**

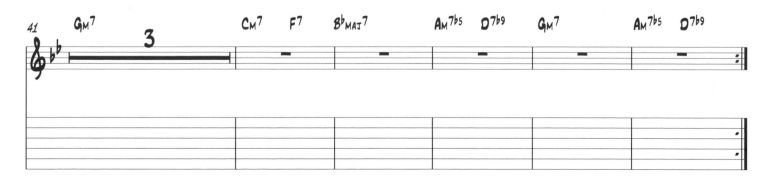

# Good Bait

## By Tadd Dameron and Count Basie

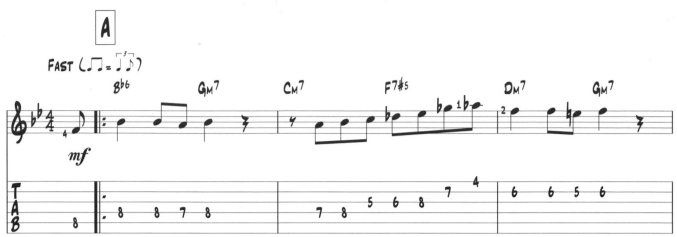

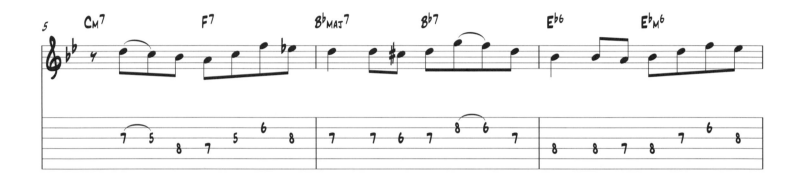

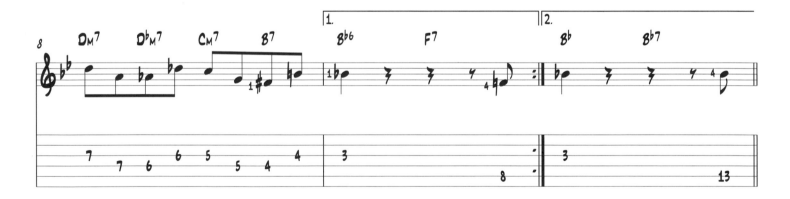

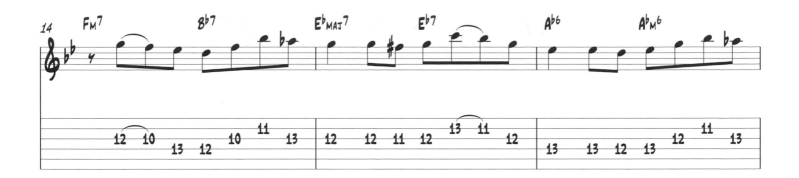

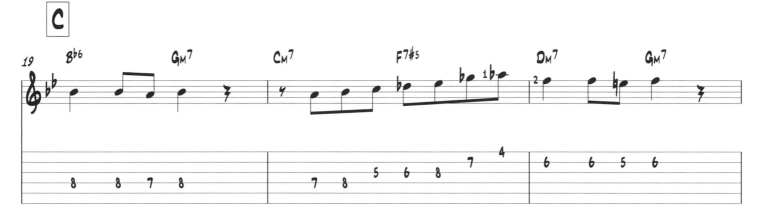

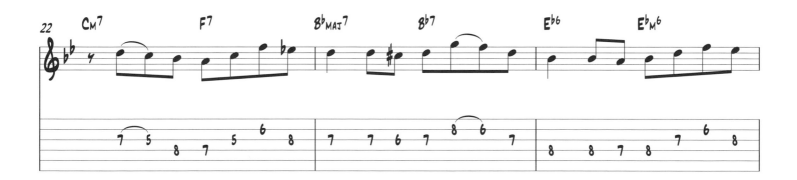

# Goodbye Pork Pie Hat

By Charles Mingus

*Played as even eighth notes.

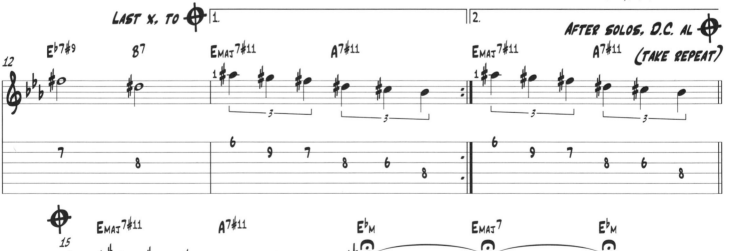

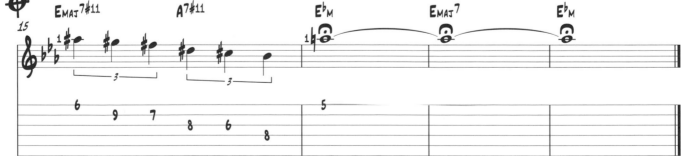

# Mr. P.C.

By John Coltrane

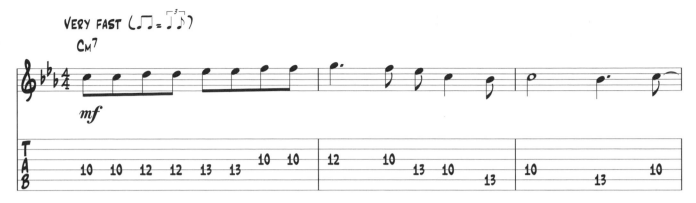

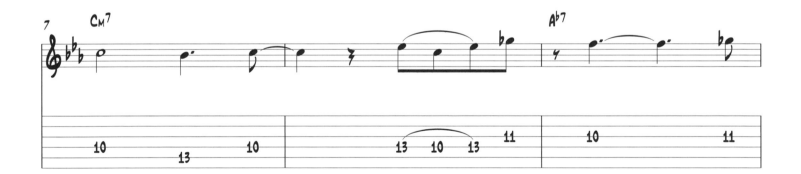

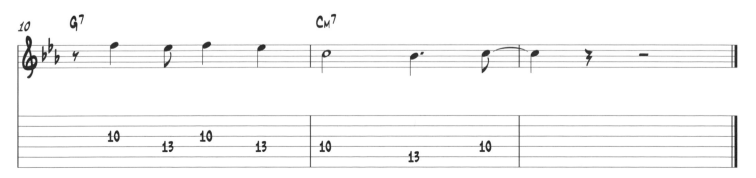

# Groovin' High

By John "Dizzy" Gillespie

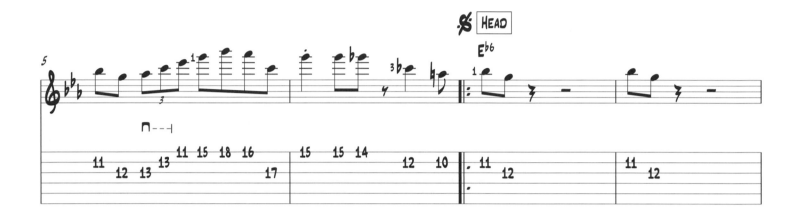

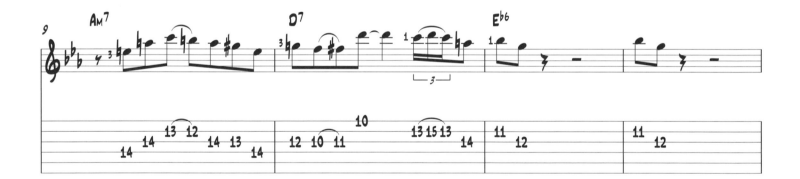

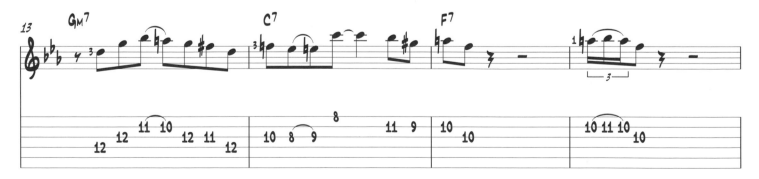

46

# Honeysuckle Rose

FROM AIN'T MISBEHAVIN'

**Words by Andy Razaf**
**Music by Thomas "Fats" Waller**

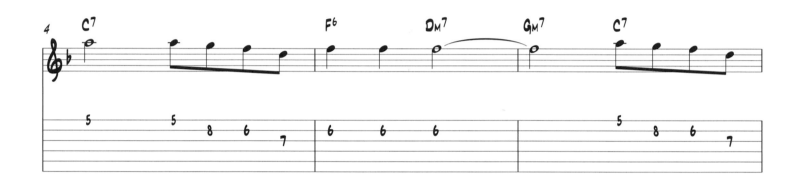

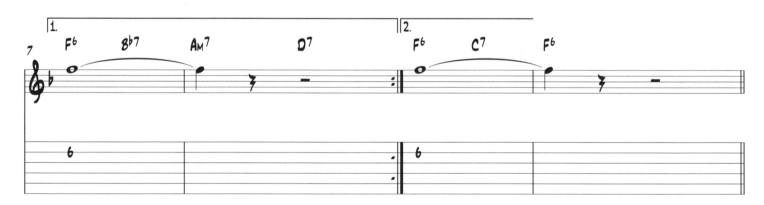

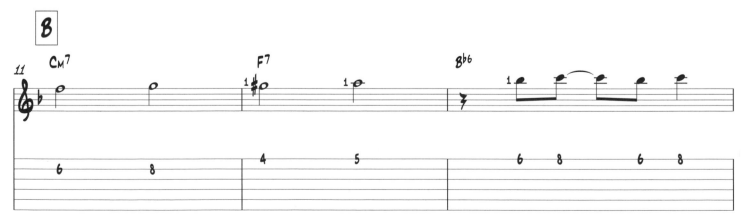

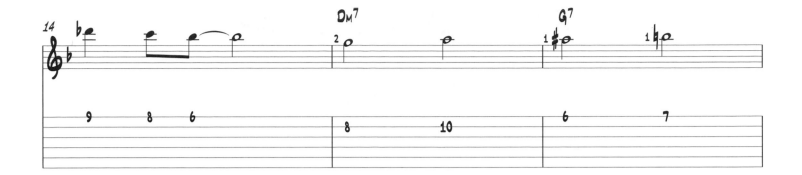

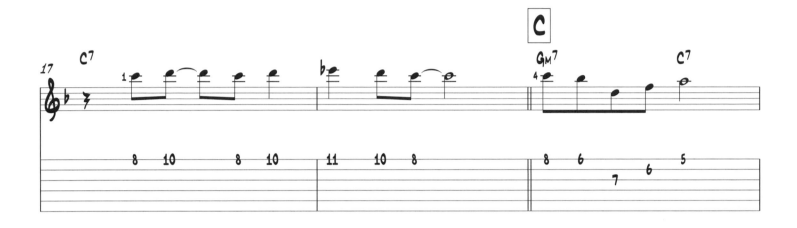

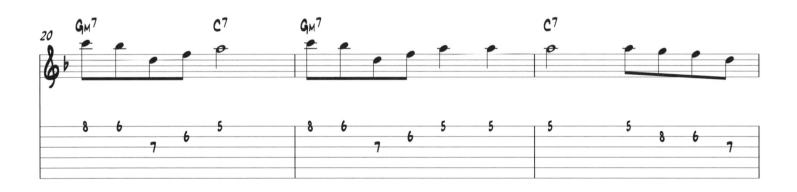

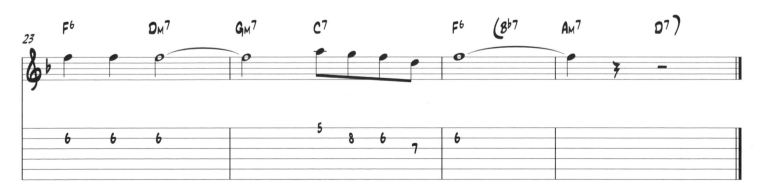

# How High the Moon

FROM *TWO FOR THE SHOW*

Lyrics by Nancy Hamilton
Music by Morgan Lewis

**A**

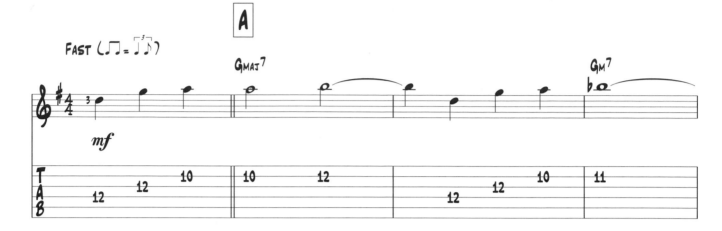

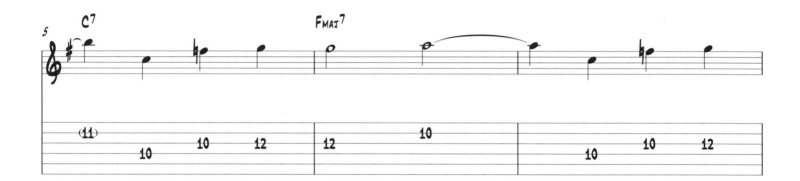

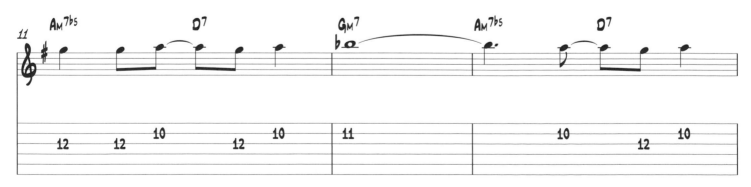

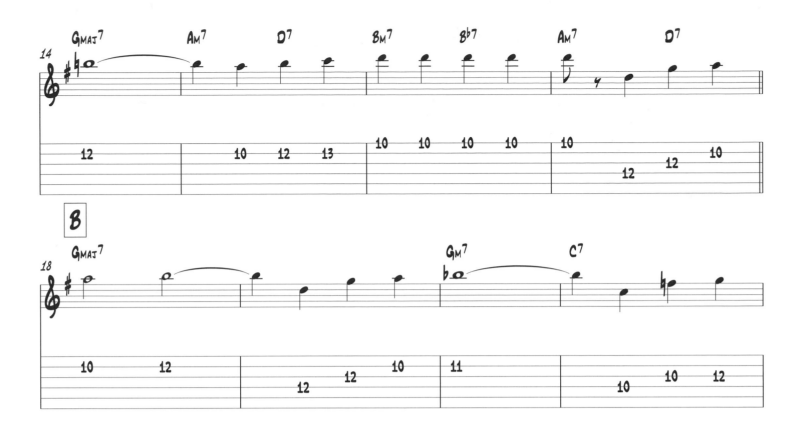

**B**

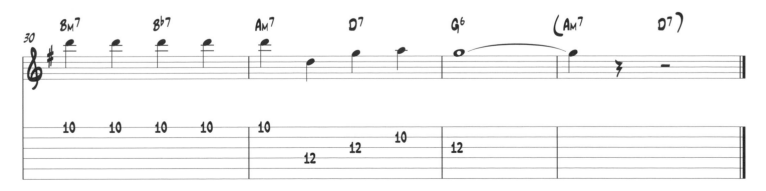

# I Got Rhythm

### from An American in Paris

### Music and Lyrics by George Gershwin and Ira Gershwin

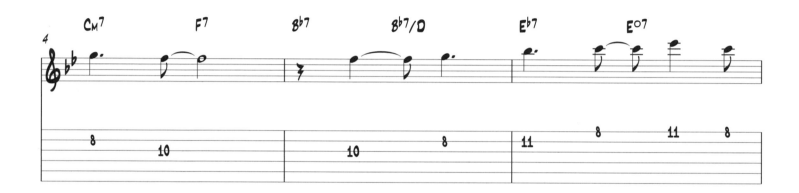

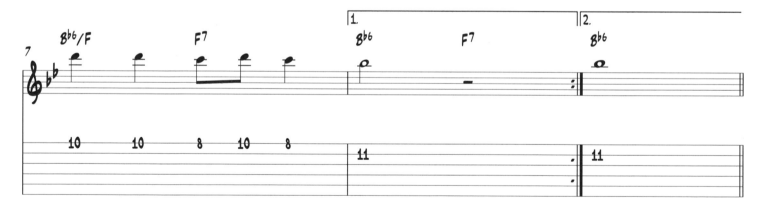

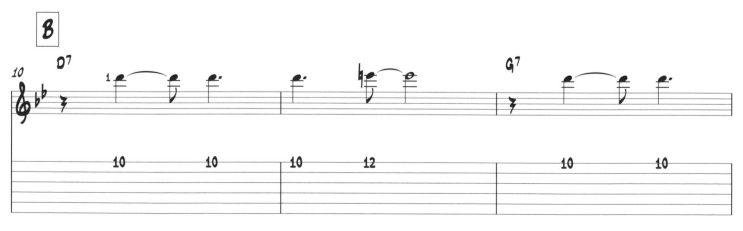

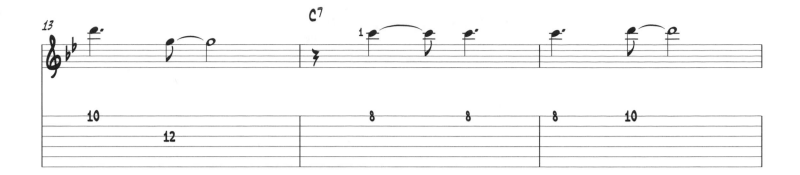

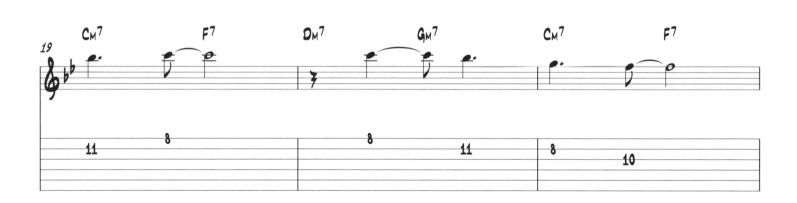

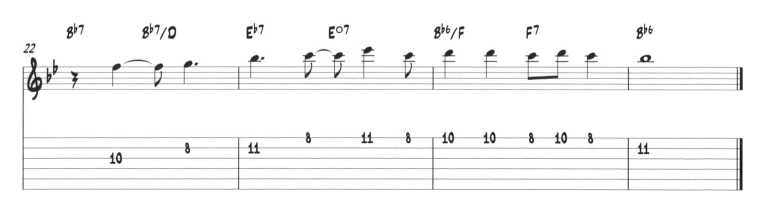

# In the Mood

By Joe Garland

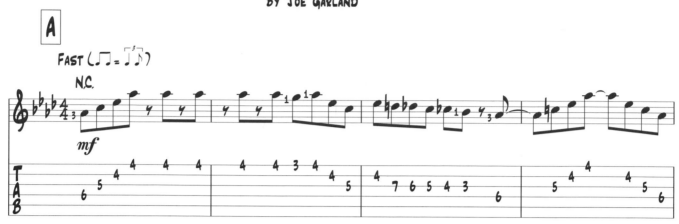

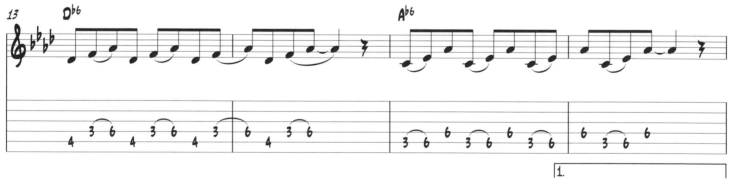

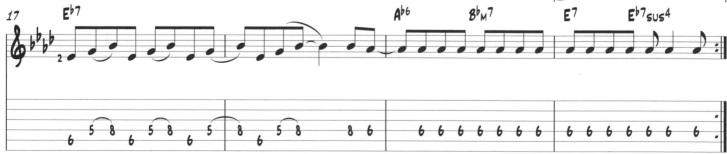

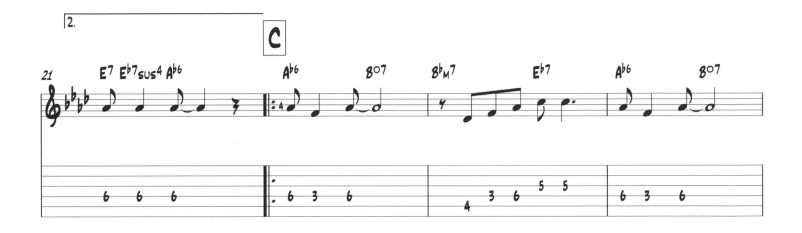

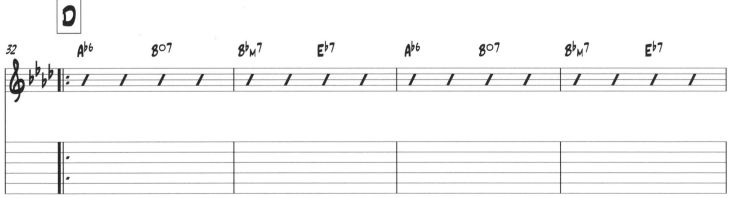

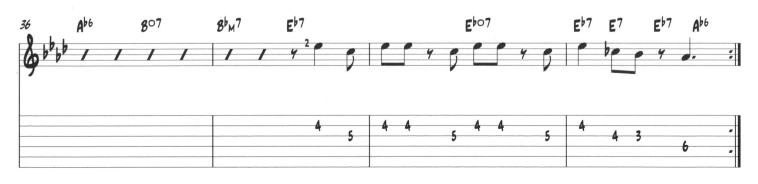

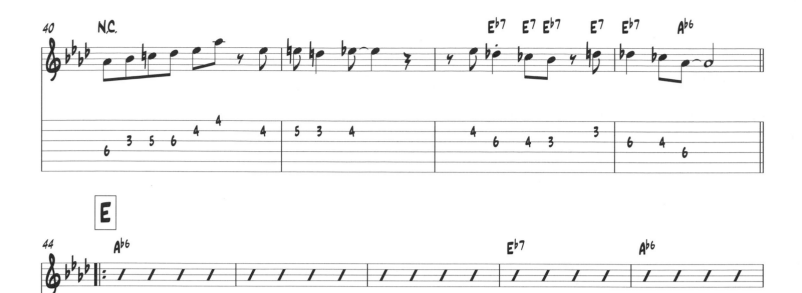

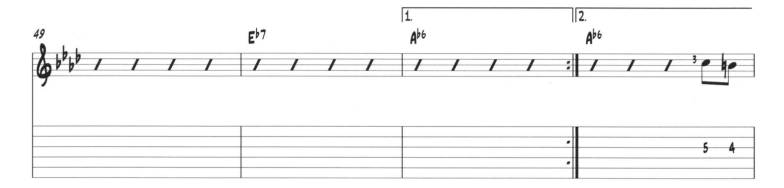

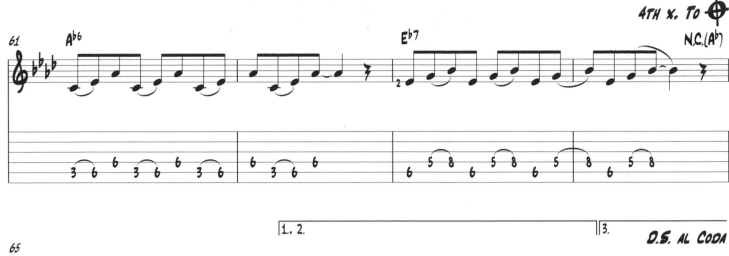

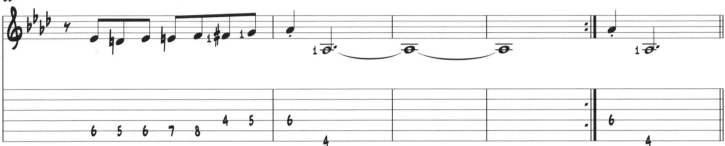

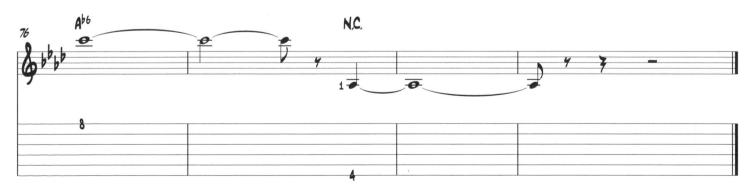

# In Walked Bud

By Thelonious Monk

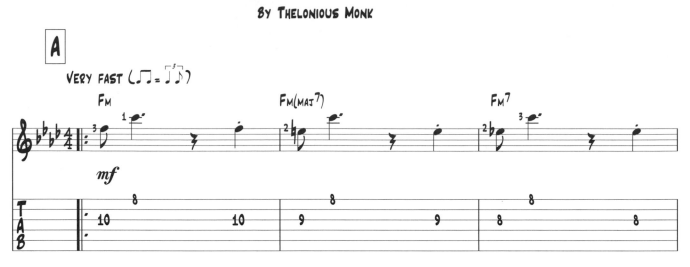

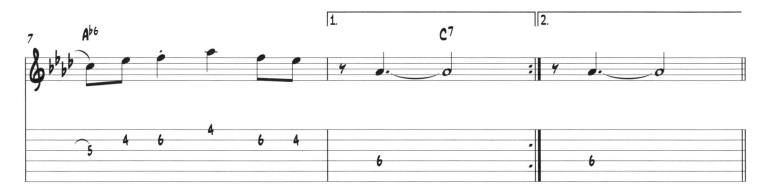

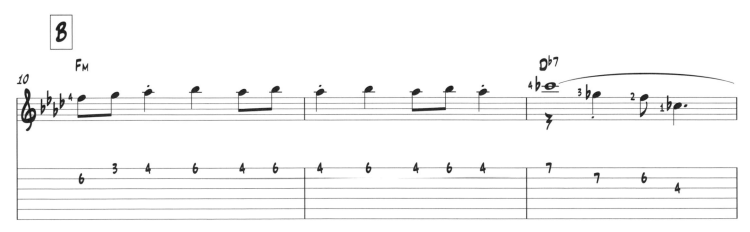

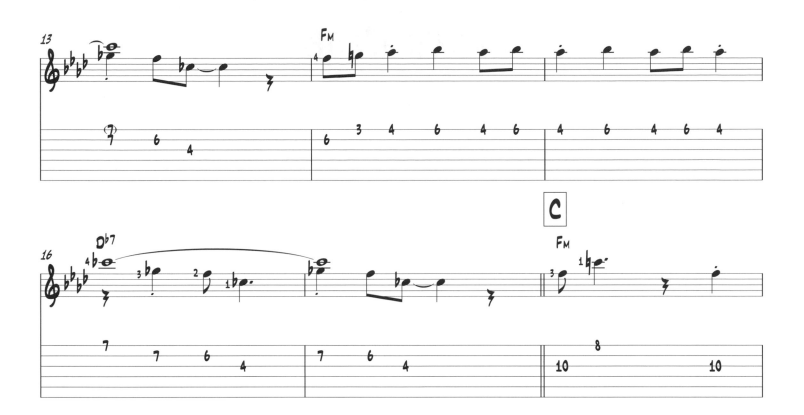

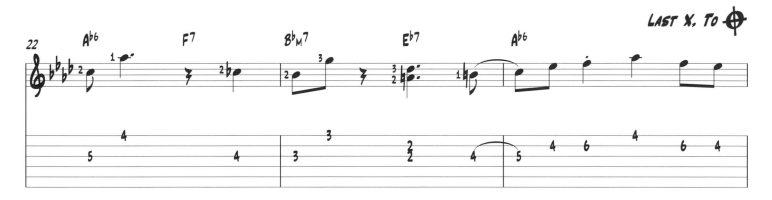

# Inner Urge

By Joe Henderson

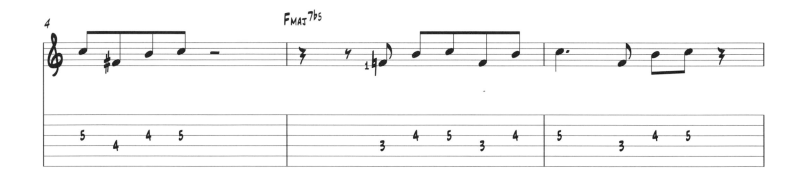

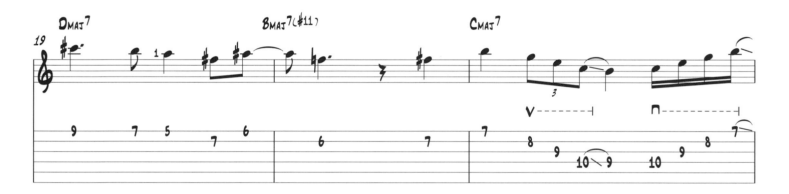

# Invitation

Words by Paul Francis Webster
Music by Bronislau Kaper

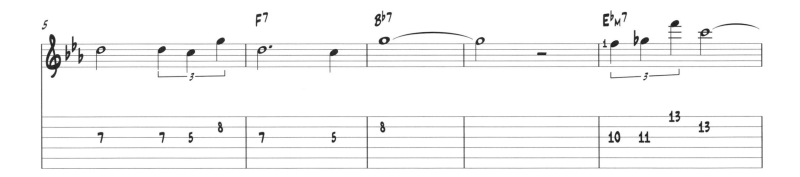

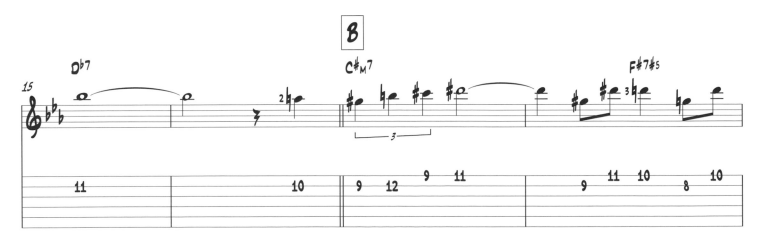

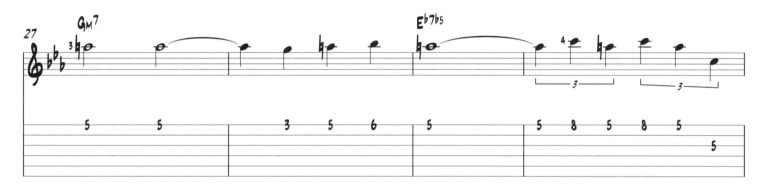

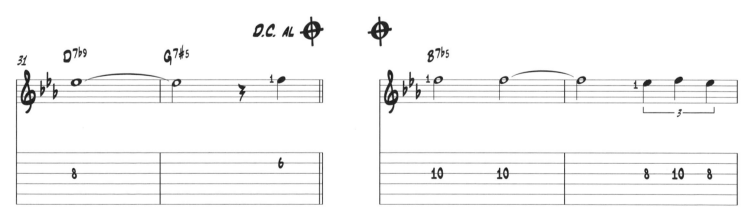

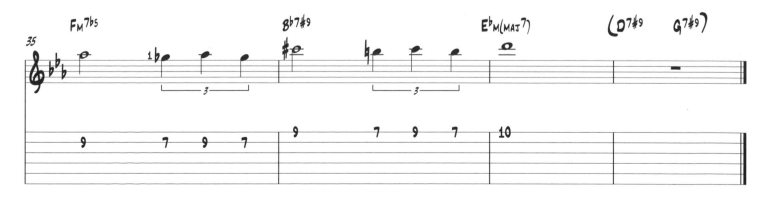

# Lullaby of Birdland

**Words by George David Weiss**
**Music by George Shearing**

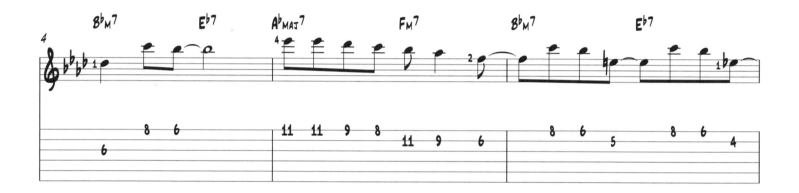

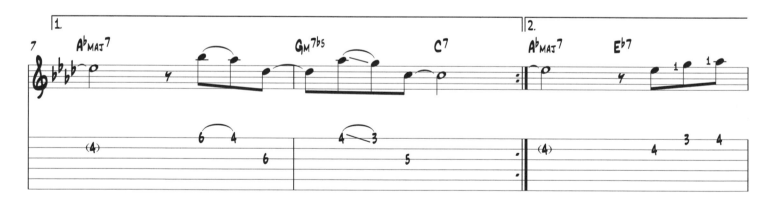

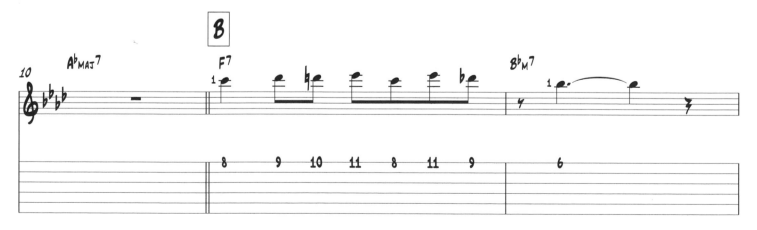

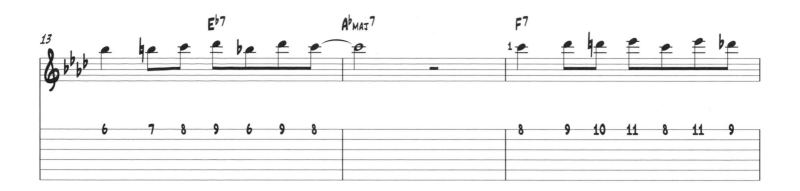

**C**

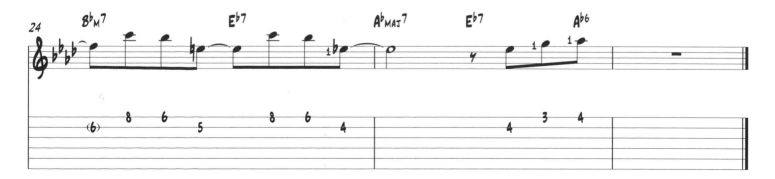

# Move

By Denzil De Costa Best

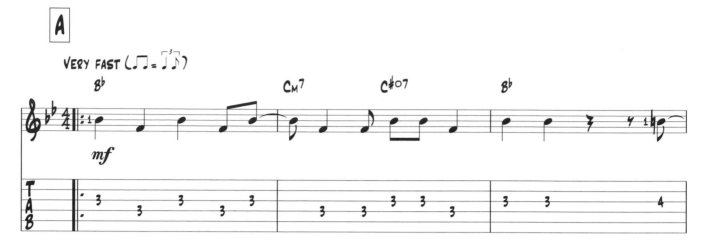

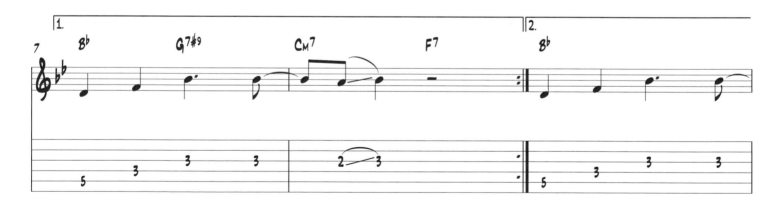

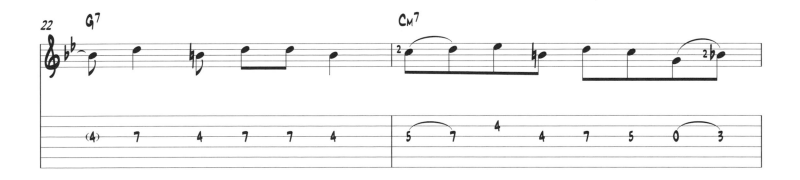

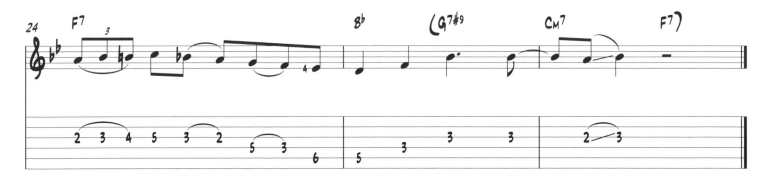

# Nardis

## BY MILES DAVIS

*W/ PICK & MIDDLE FINGER.

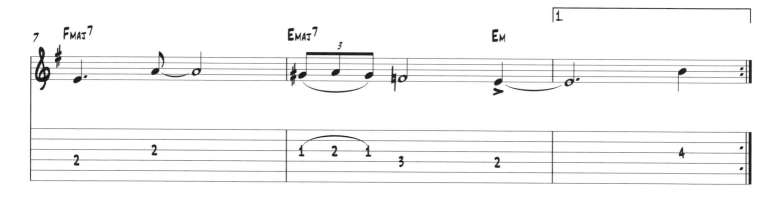

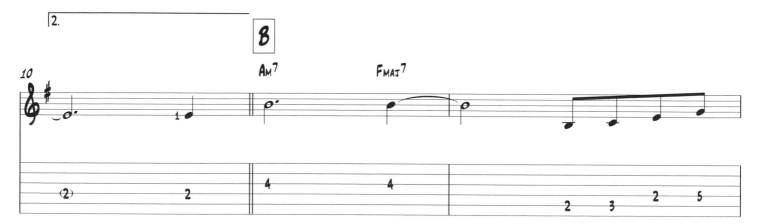

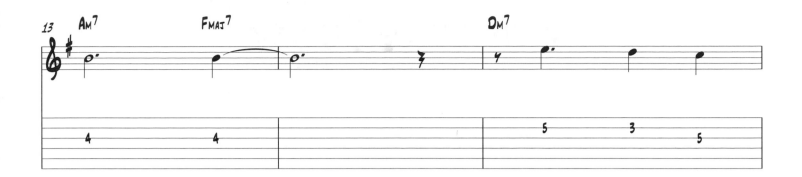

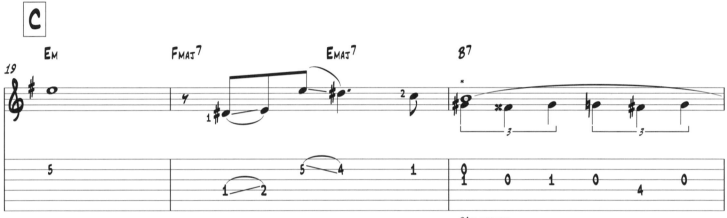

*As before

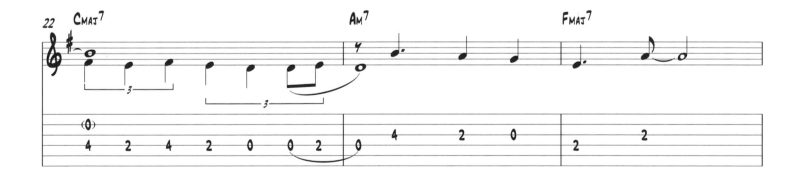

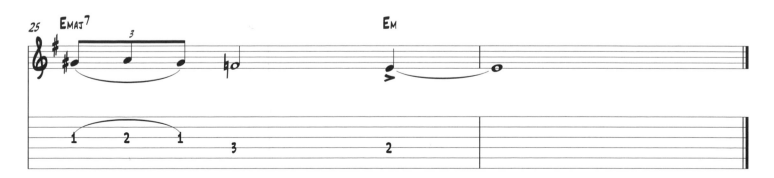

# A Night In Tunisia

By John "Dizzy" Gillespie and Frank Paparelli

*Bass arr. for gtr., next 3 meas.

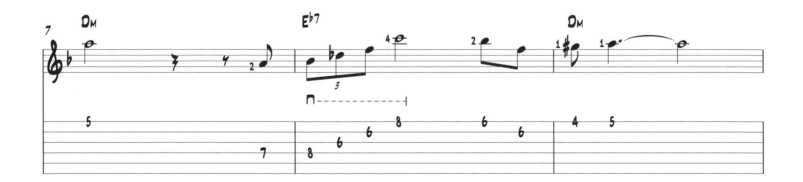

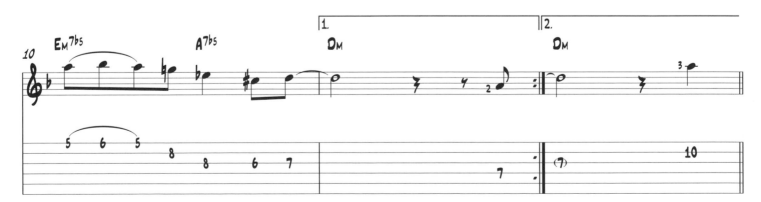

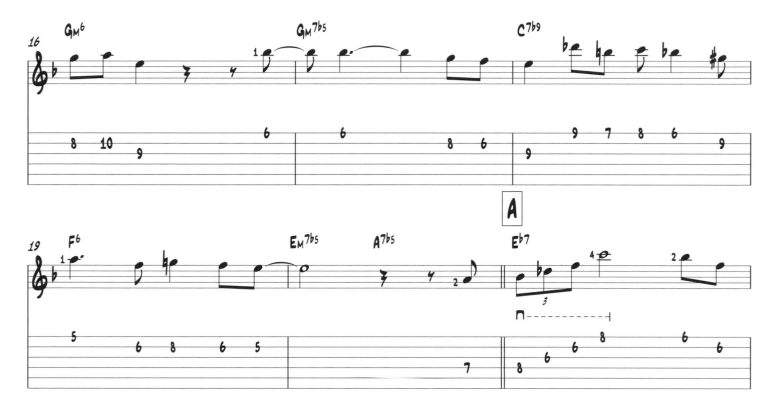

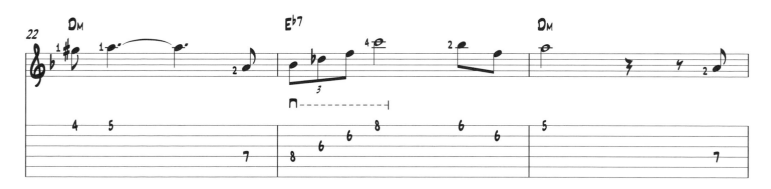

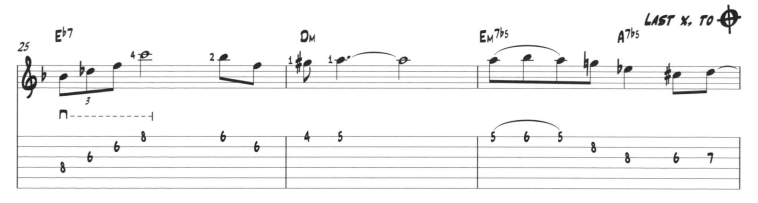

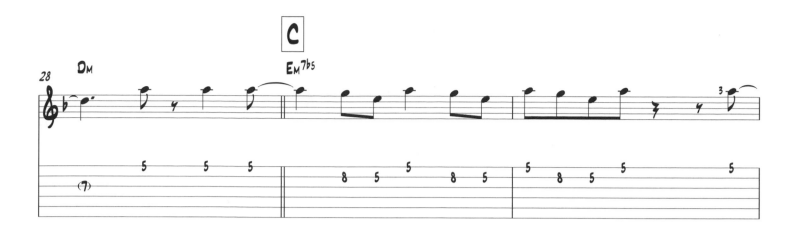

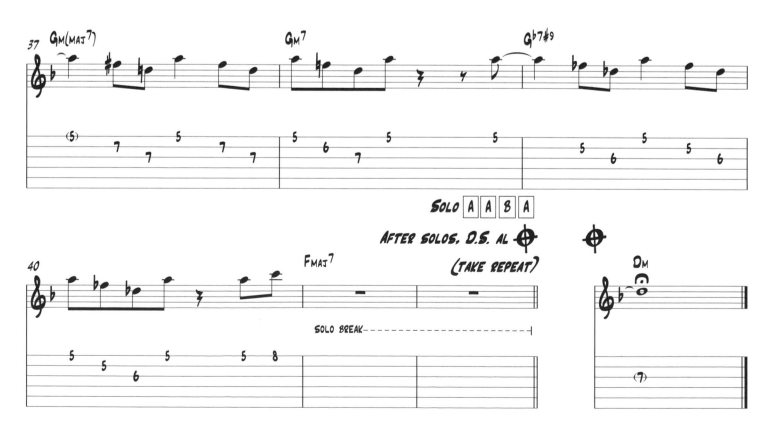

# Recorda Me

## By Joe Henderson

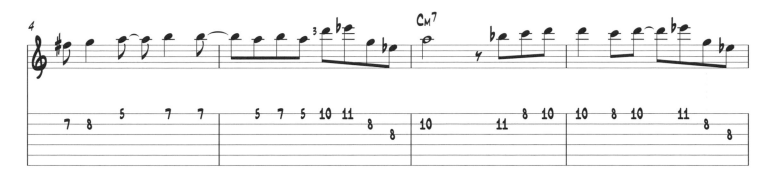

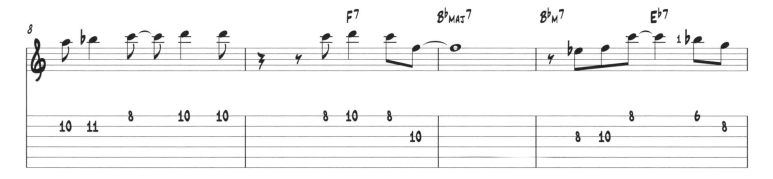

# Oleo

By Sonny Rollins

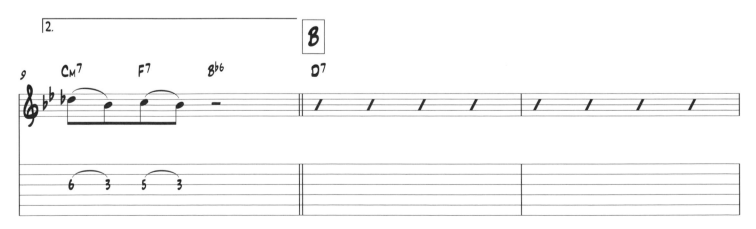

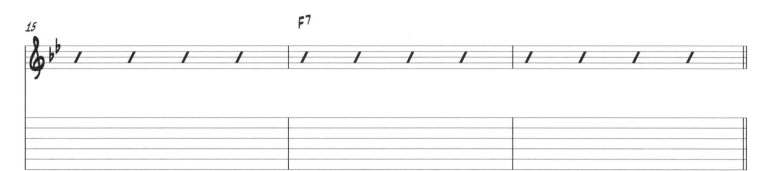

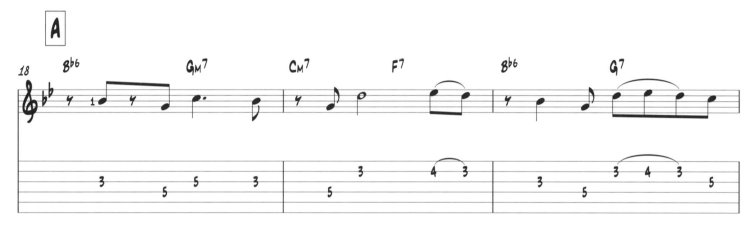

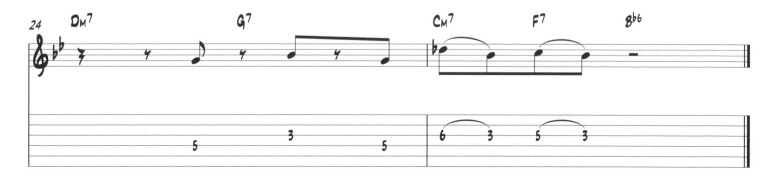

# On Green Dolphin Street

### Lyrics by Ned Washington
### Music by Bronislau Kaper

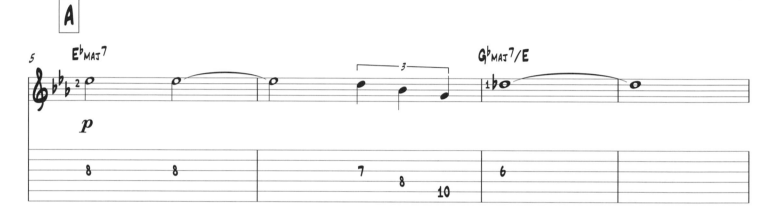

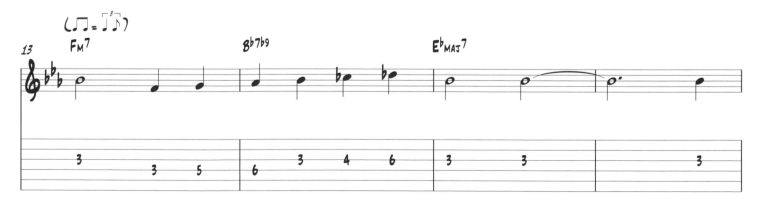

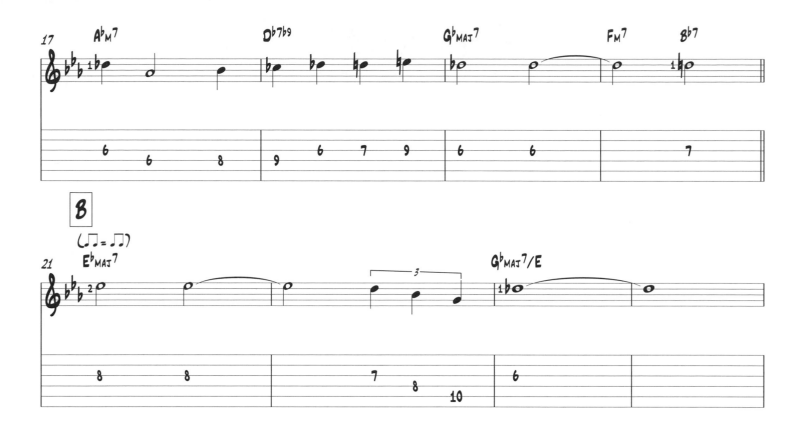

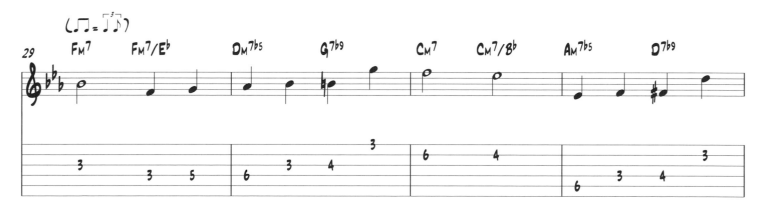

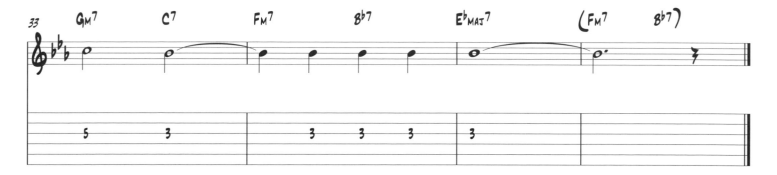

# Ornithology

By Charlie Parker and Bennie Harris

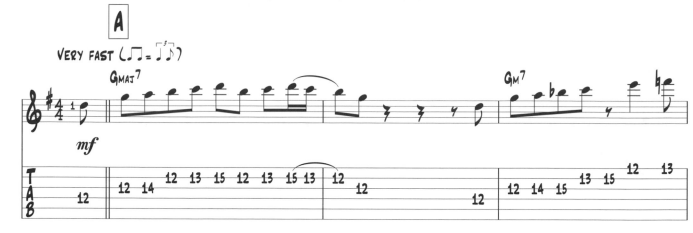

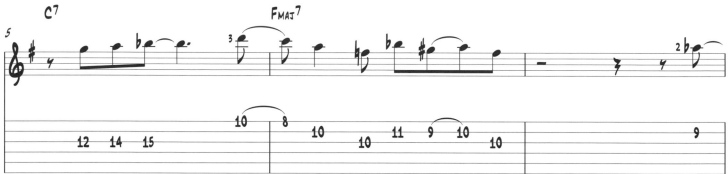

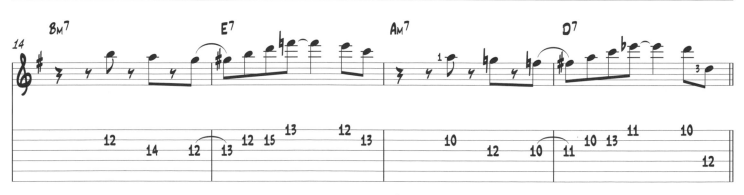

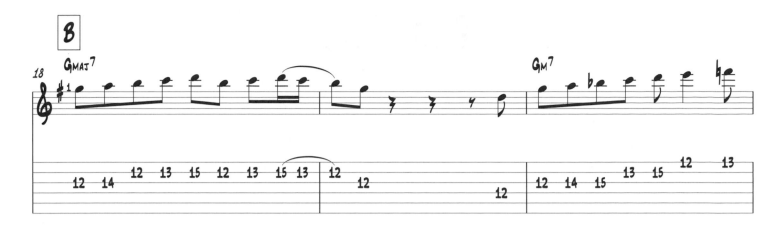

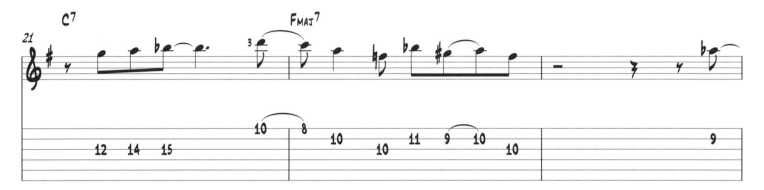

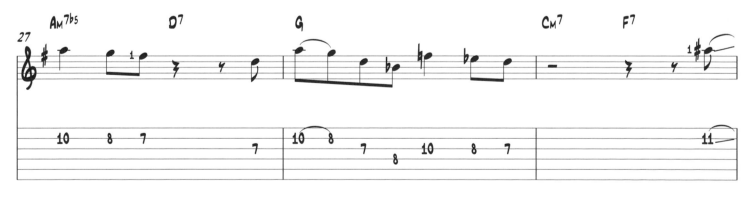

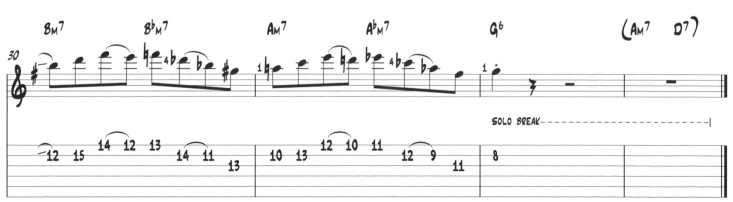

# Red Clay

By Freddie Hubbard

*Bass & keyboard arr. for gtr., next 8 meas.

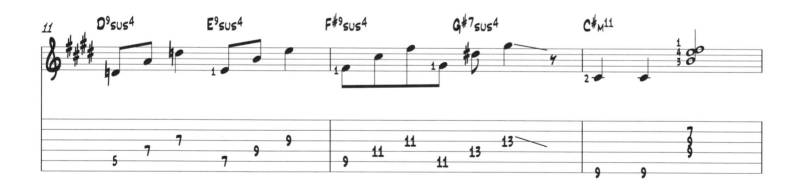

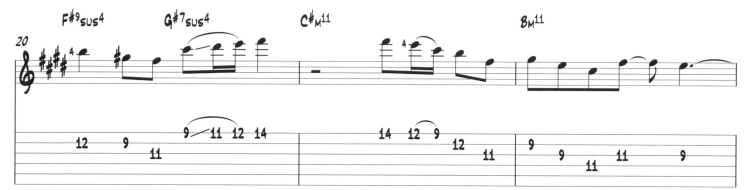

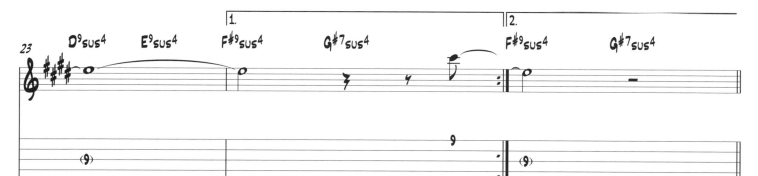

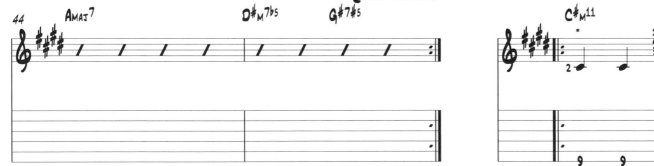

*Bass & keyboard arr. for gtr.

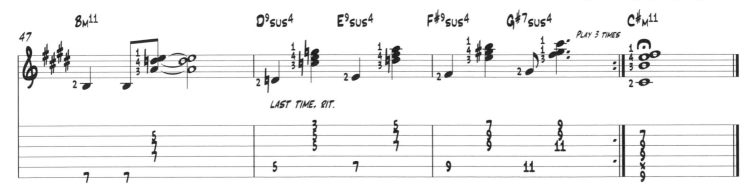

# St. Thomas

By Sonny Rollins

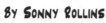

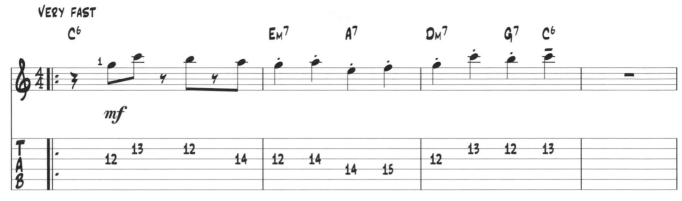

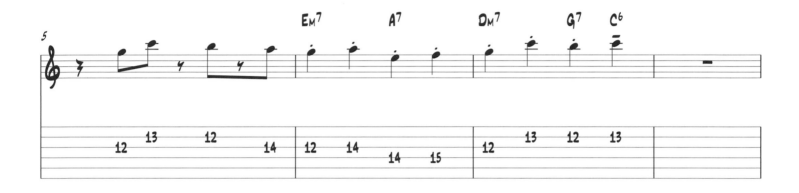

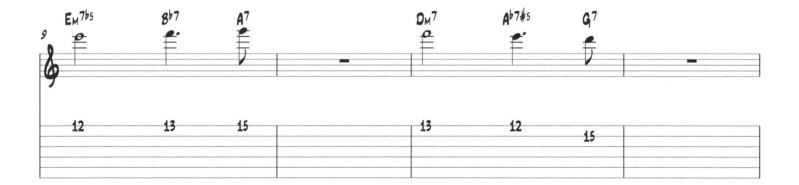

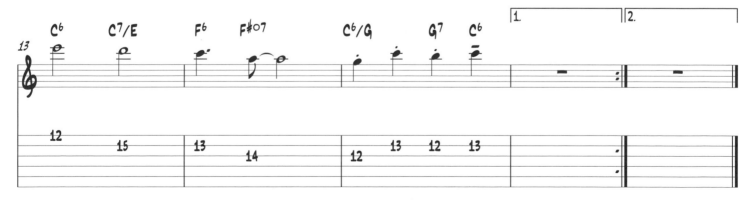

# Satin Doll

### FROM *SOPHISTICATED LADIES*
#### BY DUKE ELLINGTON

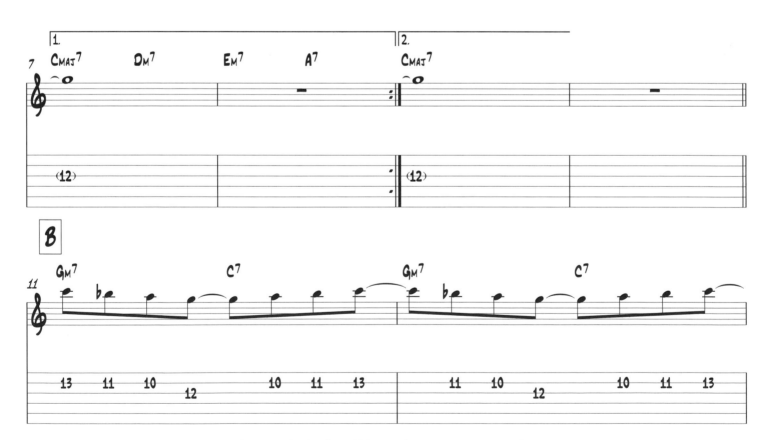

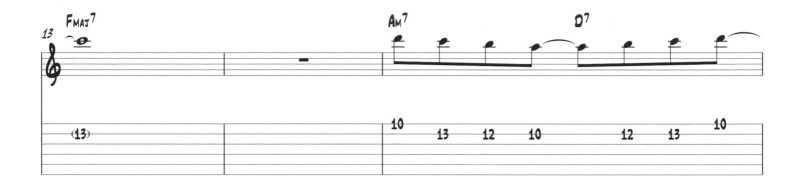

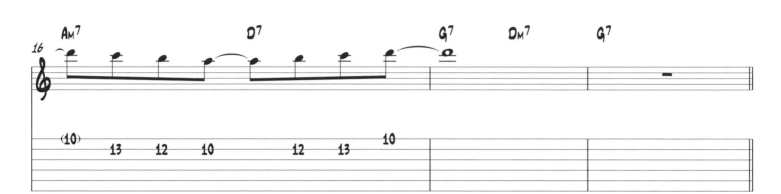

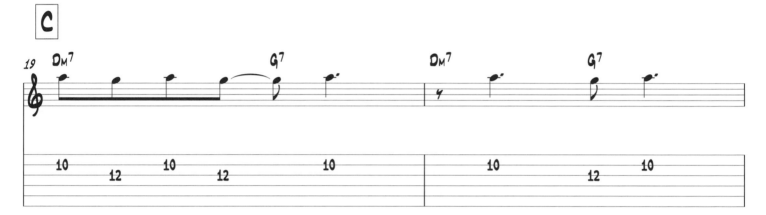

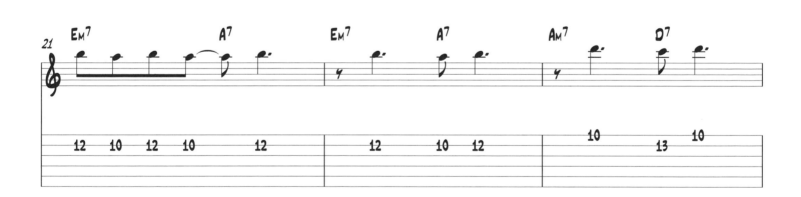

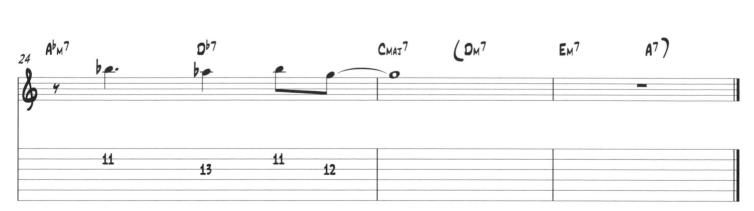

# Scrapple From The Apple

By Charlie Parker

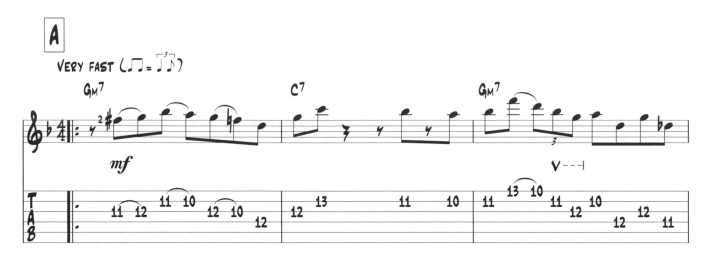

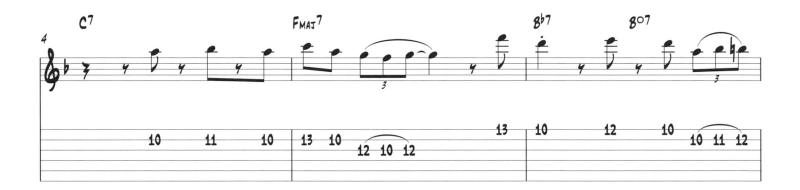

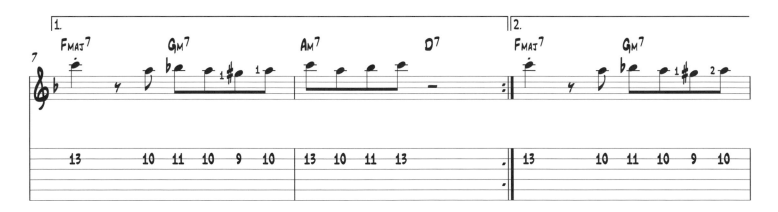

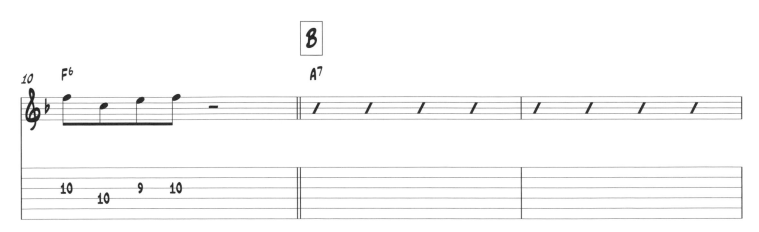

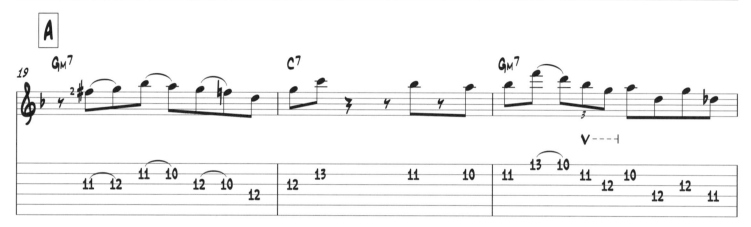

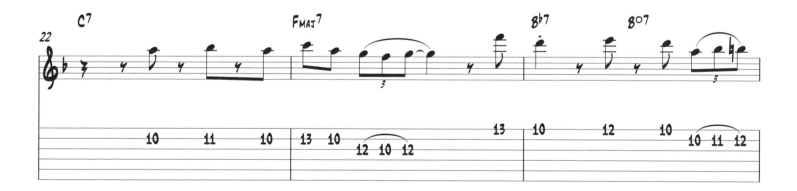

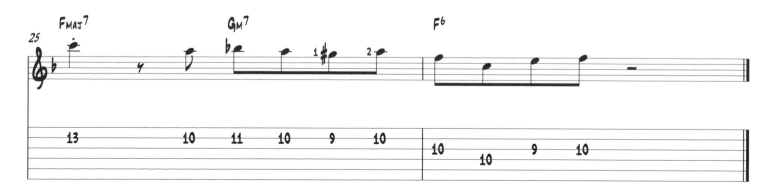

# Song for My Father

## Words and Music by Horace Silver

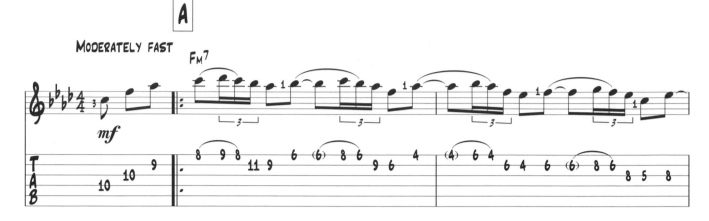

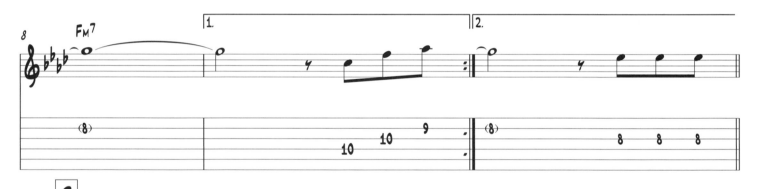

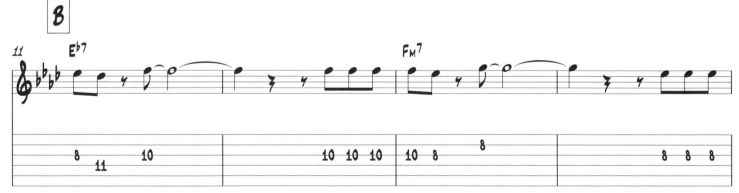

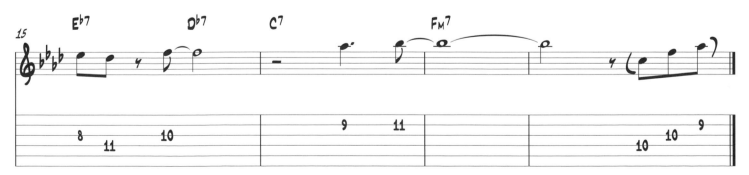

# Sugar

By Stanley Turrentine

# Stolen Moments

### Words and Music by Oliver Nelson

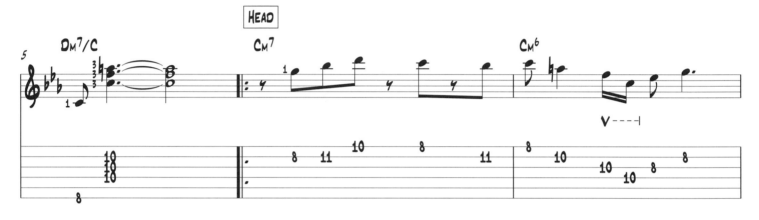

*Bass & Horns arr. for gtr. next 4 meas.

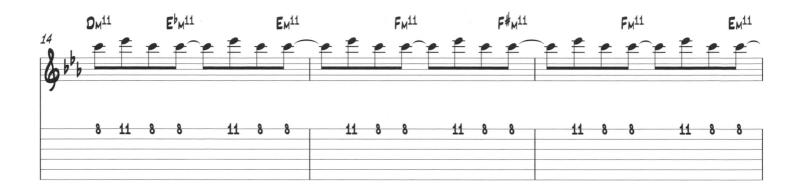

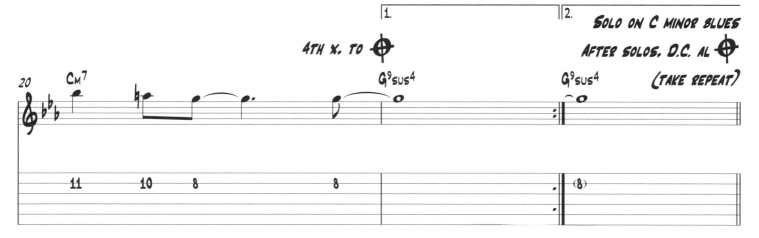

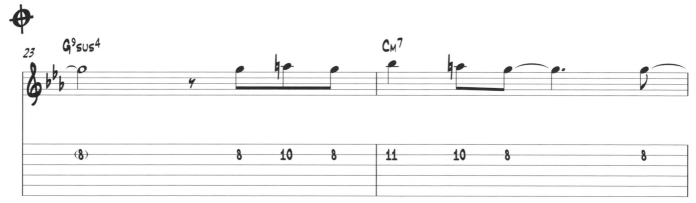

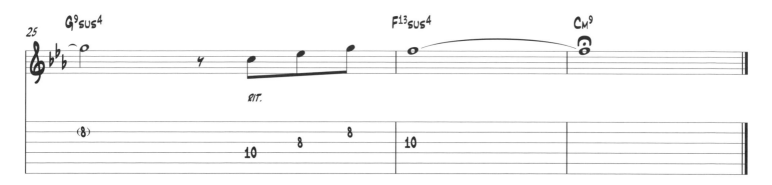

# Take Five

By Paul Desmond

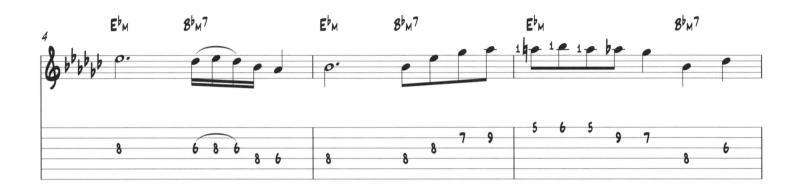

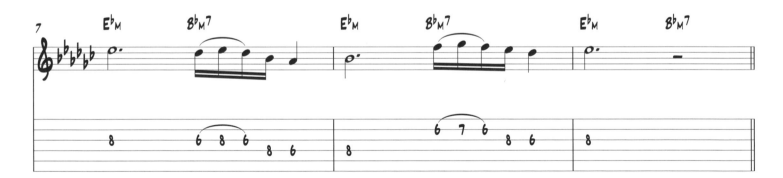

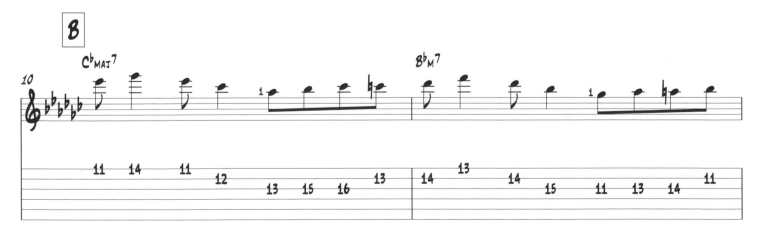

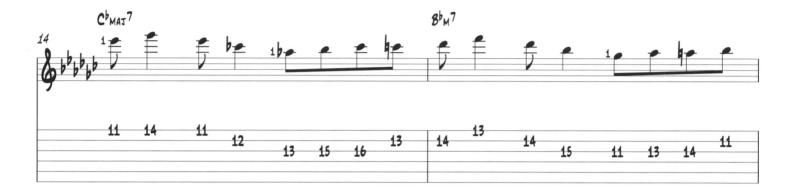

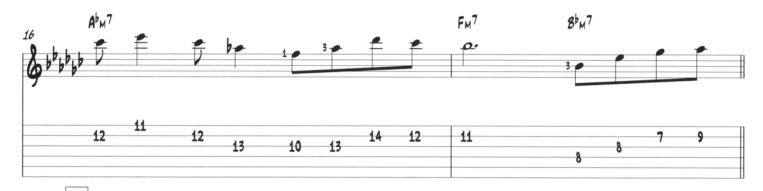

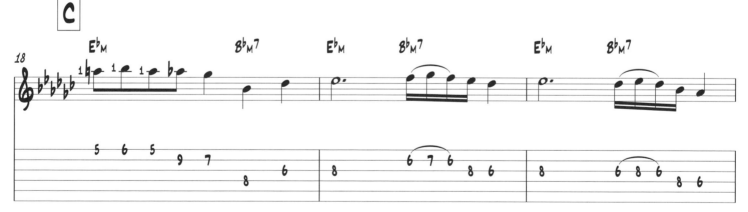

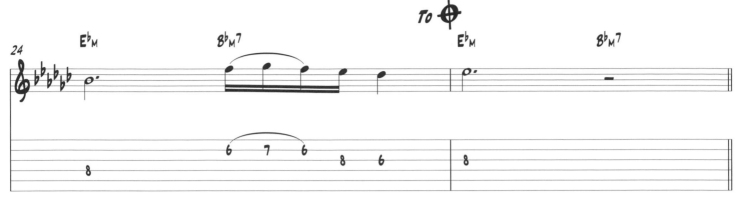

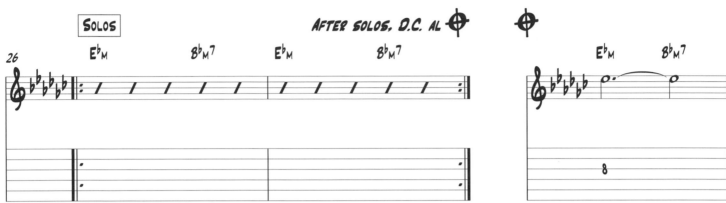

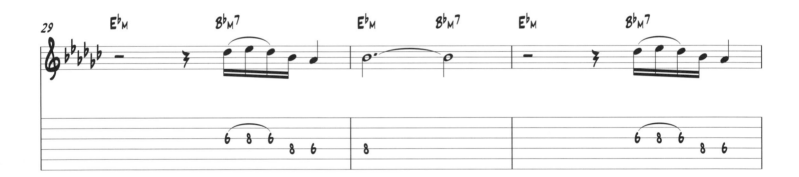

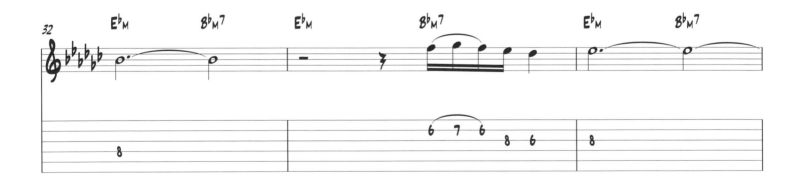

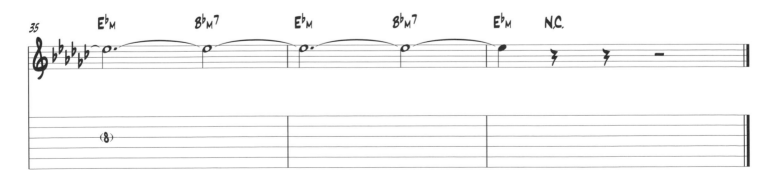

# Tenor Madness

By Sonny Rollins

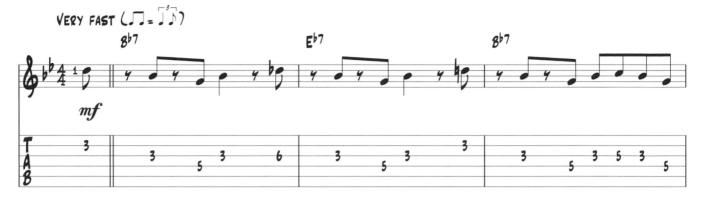

# There Will Never Be Another You

FROM THE MOTION PICTURE ICELAND

LYRIC BY MACK GORDON
MUSIC BY HARRY WARREN

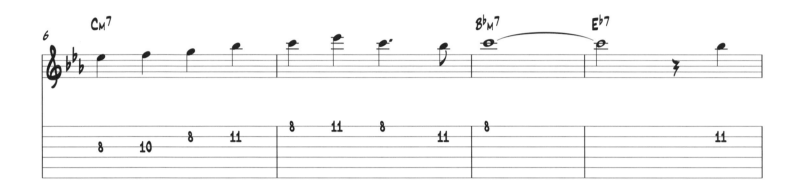

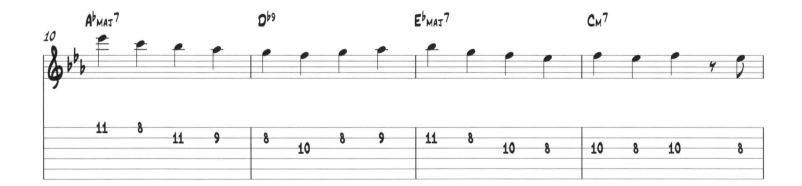

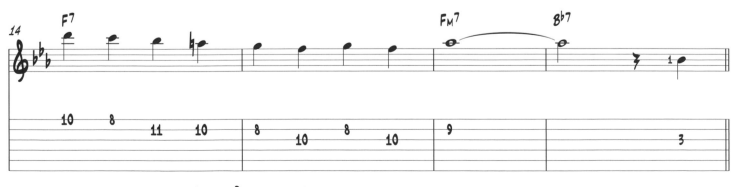

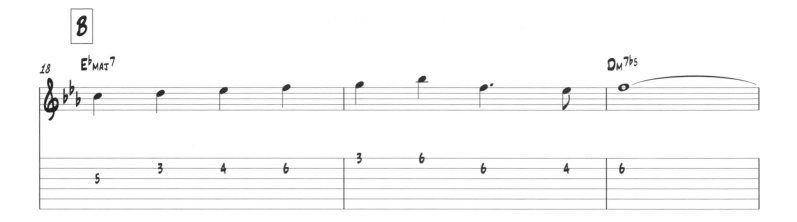

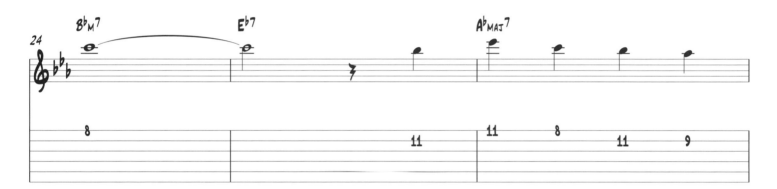

# Well You Needn't
## (It's Over Now)

Words by Mike Ferro
Music by Thelonious Monk

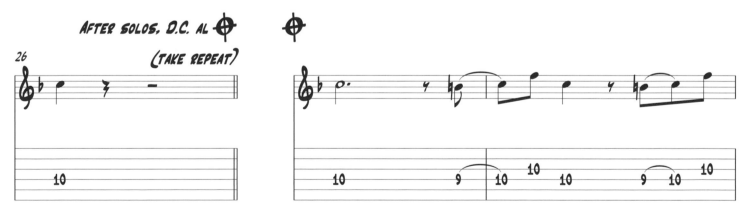

# Whisper Not

By Benny Golson

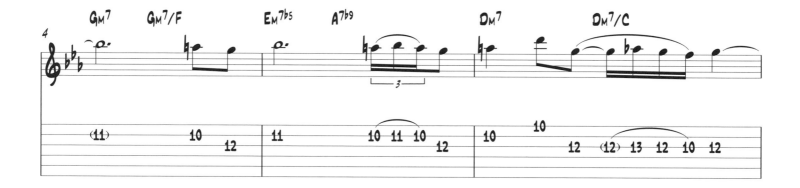

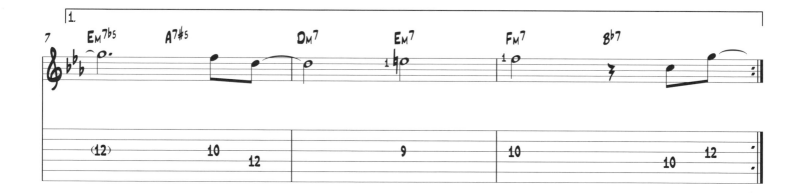

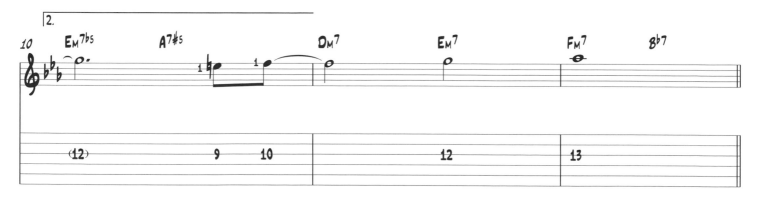

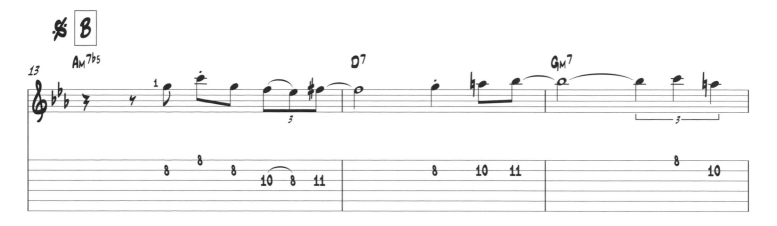

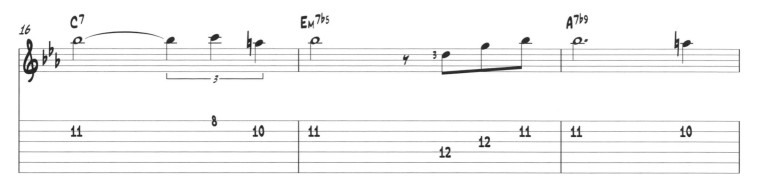

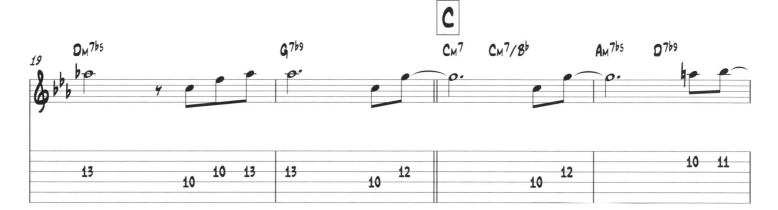

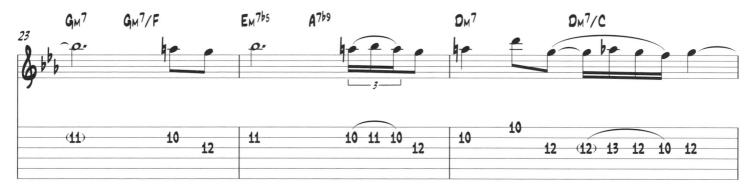

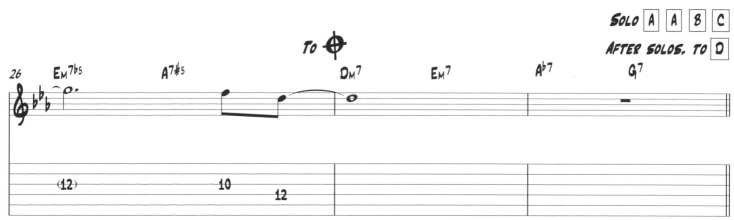

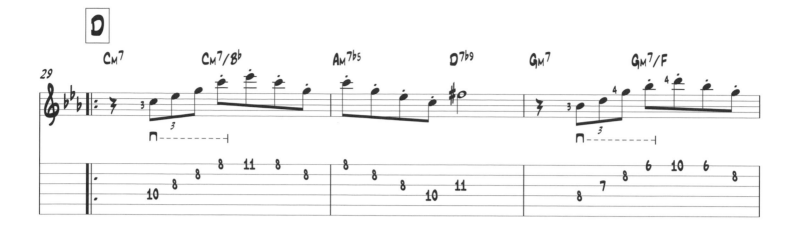

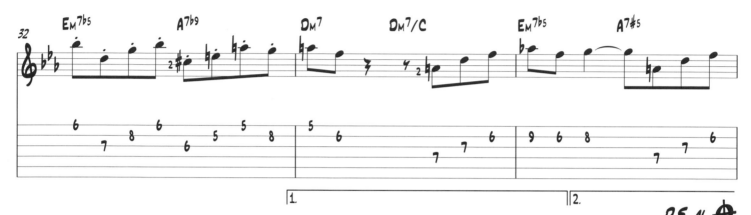

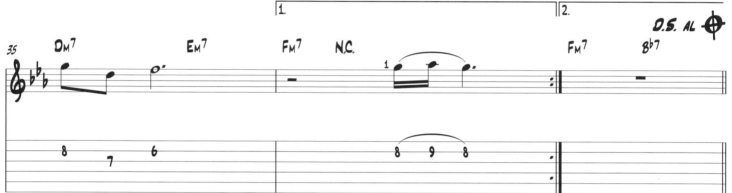

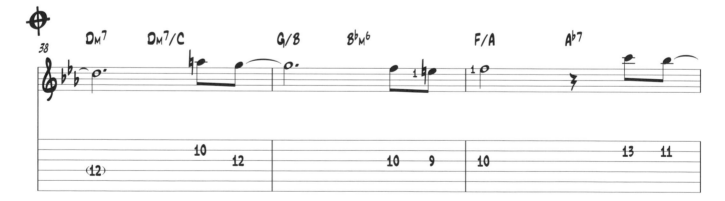

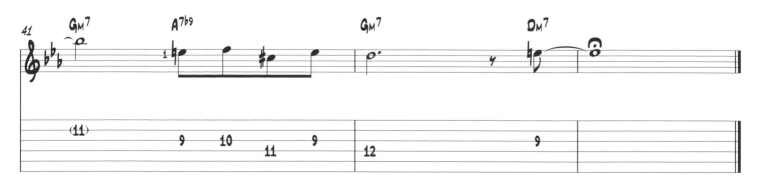

# GUITAR NOTATION LEGEND

Guitar music can be notated three different ways: on a *musical staff*, in *tablature*, and in *rhythm slashes*.

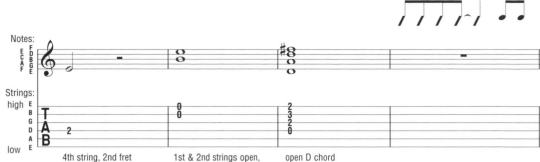

**RHYTHM SLASHES** are written above the staff. Strum chords in the rhythm indicated. Use the chord diagrams found at the top of the first page of the transcription for the appropriate chord voicings. Round noteheads indicate single notes.

**THE MUSICAL STAFF** shows pitches and rhythms and is divided by bar lines into measures. Pitches are named after the first seven letters of the alphabet.

**TABLATURE** graphically represents the guitar fingerboard. Each horizontal line represents a string, and each number represents a fret.

4th string, 2nd fret     1st & 2nd strings open, played together     open D chord

**HALF-STEP BEND:** Strike the note and bend up 1/2 step.

**WHOLE-STEP BEND:** Strike the note and bend up one step.

**GRACE NOTE BEND:** Strike the note and immediately bend up as indicated.

**SLIGHT (MICROTONE) BEND:** Strike the note and bend up 1/4 step.

**BEND AND RELEASE:** Strike the note and bend up as indicated, then release back to the original note. Only the first note is struck.

**PRE-BEND:** Bend the note as indicated, then strike it.

**VIBRATO:** The string is vibrated by rapidly bending and releasing the note with the fretting hand.

**WIDE VIBRATO:** The pitch is varied to a greater degree by vibrating with the fretting hand.

**HAMMER-ON:** Strike the first (lower) note with one finger, then sound the higher note (on the same string) with another finger by fretting it without picking.

**PULL-OFF:** Place both fingers on the notes to be sounded. Strike the first note and without picking, pull the finger off to sound the second (lower) note.

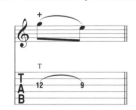

**LEGATO SLIDE:** Strike the first note and then slide the same fret-hand finger up or down to the second note. The second note is not struck.

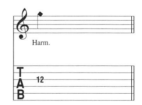

**SHIFT SLIDE:** Same as legato slide, except the second note is struck.

**TRILL:** Very rapidly alternate between the notes indicated by continuously hammering on and pulling off.

**TAPPING:** Hammer ("tap") the fret indicated with the pick-hand index or middle finger and pull off to the note fretted by the fret hand.

**NATURAL HARMONIC:** Strike the note while the fret-hand lightly touches the string directly over the fret indicated.

**PINCH HARMONIC:** The note is fretted normally and a harmonic is produced by adding the edge of the thumb or the tip of the index finger of the pick hand to the normal pick attack.

**PICK SCRAPE:** The edge of the pick is rubbed down (or up) the string, producing a scratchy sound.

**MUFFLED STRINGS:** A percussive sound is produced by laying the fret hand across the string(s) without depressing, and striking them with the pick hand.

**PALM MUTING:** The note is partially muted by the pick hand lightly touching the string(s) just before the bridge.

**RAKE:** Drag the pick across the strings indicated with a single motion.

**TREMOLO PICKING:** The note is picked as rapidly and continuously as possible.

**VIBRATO BAR DIVE AND RETURN:** The pitch of the note or chord is dropped a specified number of steps (in rhythm), then returned to the original pitch.

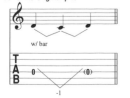

**VIBRATO BAR SCOOP:** Depress the bar just before striking the note, then quickly release the bar.

**VIBRATO BAR DIP:** Strike the note and then immediately drop a specified number of steps, then release back to the original pitch.